Contributors from the inner circle:

Joan Baker
Stephen Newman
Don LaFontaine
Fred Collins
Steve Zirnkilton
Joe Cipriano
George DelHoyo
Sylvia Villagran
Cedering Fox
EG Daly
Keith David
Valerie Smaldone
Janice Pendarvis
Rodd Houston
Bill Ratner
Les Marshak
Hattie Winston
Nancy Giles
Dave Fennoy

Secrets
of
Voice-Over Success

Top Voice-Over Actors Reveal How They Did It

Secrets of

Voice-Over Success

First Sentient Publications edition 2005
Copyright © 2005 by Joan Baker

A paperback original

Cover design by Kiyoharu Goto
Book design by Nicholas Cummings

Library of Congress Cataloging-in-Publication Data

Baker, Joan.
  Secrets of voice-over success : top voice-over artists reveal how they did it / by Joan Baker.~ 1st Sentient Publications ed.
      p. cm.
   Includes index.
   ISBN 1-59181-033-7
   1. Television announcing~Vocational guidance. 2. Radio announcing~Vocational guidance. 3. Voice-overs. 4. Voice actors and actresses~United States~Biography. I. Title.
   PN1990.9.A54B35 2005
   792.02'8'023~dc22
                                                                                  2005002371

Printed in the United States of America

10 9 8 7 6 5 4 3 2 1

SENTIENT PUBLICATIONS
A Limited Liability Company
1113 Spruce Street
Boulder, CO 80302
www.sentientpublications.com

Secrets of

Voice-Over Success

Top Voice-Over Artists
Reveal How They Did It

Joan Baker

SENTIENT PUBLICATIONS

Dedication

THE ORIGINAL TITLE OF THIS BOOK WAS TO BE ROOM WITH A VOICE. IT IS important to explain this because it was indeed the original inspiration and perhaps the single most important reason so many outstanding voice actors signed on to contribute to this work. To explain, as a working voice-over artist, not to mention being a very self-expressed woman, I was never so moved by appreciation for my voice—the human voice—as when Alzheimer's disease claimed the voice of my father before finally claiming his life. I still see him there, sitting, more or less immobilized, in a sparsely furnished room without the use of the powerful voice that once delivered his every intention with so much vigor it made me want to swim in the sound. Watching him, it occurred to me that much of my life as a voice-over artist is also spent alone in a room, a "room with a voice." This physically and (to a large degree) emotionally describes our careers as voice-over artists—time spent alone in a room with *our* voices—a soundproof door shut tight making all too tangible the dead silence in the confines of a small physical space. But in that space and from within that silence we come alive, probing for the interpretations that will give meaning to the words— crafting those words into our own with impact and emotion, aiming them, motivating others to understanding and action. In our room we break the silence and give robust voice to feelings. I can rain my sound down on the microphone so that the outside world knows my full expression.

Sadly, people with the disease known as Alzheimer's find themselves existing in an oddly parallel world, often isolated in their rooms (and conditions) with slowly deteriorating bodies and minds, struggling in their physical space as victims, succumbing to an ever-growing stalking silence ... until inevitably unable to express words (for many have lost their meaning) or even sounds. A room with *no* voice is all that remains. I lamented how tragic it was that my dad could no longer express himself, when it occurred to me in a completely new way. I saw that in my father's room, even as he sat physically unable to form words, I was—through some miracle of kindred consciousness, through some marvel of fatherly lessons imbued in me as a child—able to hear his voice, the voice he set free in the world through the powerful way he lived in it, with every nuance of purpose, every thoughtful concern, every expression of love.

And how fitting it is that a community of voice-over actors who depend on being self-expressed for their very livelihood would in turn honor those who no longer can. This book and its original title, *Room with a Voice*, is dedicated to my dad, James Palmer Baker, and to all those who lived and do live with Alzheimer's. All of my proceeds from the sale of this book will be entirely contributed to the Alzheimer's Association for a cure.

Special Gratitude

My deepest love and gratitude go to my loving husband, Rudy Gaskins.

Words could not describe the impact of your ever-loving support to me. You have my immeasurable appreciation for your remarkable insights, transformative vision, and profound inspiration, which piloted the achievement and spirit of this book, brought to life my dream of contributing something positive in the world, and integrated the gift of a daughter longing to acknowledge her father's strength in her life.

I'll never forget what a powerful force you have been, sharing your genius with me every day, every hour, every moment, every step of the way. I love you.

Joan

Acknowledgments

IT IS WITH GREAT HUMILITY AND JOY THAT I ACKNOWLEDGE LANDMARK Education in New York City for the invaluable education it has provided me toward the realization and creation of this book. That this book was born out of love and the desire to contribute to humanity is the direct result of my being touched, moved, and inspired by Landmark's training. In the process of bringing this project to fruition, thousands already have been enlightened about the opportunity to eradicate Alzheimer's disease. Now, with the book's completion, I'm enthusiastic that hundreds of thousands more will be encouraged about the profound possibility of a cure—a possibility that gives each of us security for the future.

My heartfelt thanks to the following people who facilitated securing voice-over talent for my book: Wes Stevens—Vox; Robyn Stecher—Don Buchwald and Associates; Shari Hoffman—Innovative Artists; Vanessa Gilbert—Tisherman Agency; Donna Mancino—Cunningham, Escott, Slevin & Dipene; Rita Vennari—Sutton, Barth & Vennari; Marci Polzin—Innovative Artists LA; and Vickie Barroso—Paradigm.

Blowing kisses to: Michael Bond; Cedering Fox; Joel January; Sharlene Martin; Stan Baker; Meredith Berke of Push Creative; and Nancy Johnston, Director of Outreach Services of McCormick Home.

My profound thanks to the following people who inspired and encouraged me along the way with my book: Scott Hathaway, Gary Hochberg, Johnna Gottlieb—Johnna Gottlieb Consulting, Richard Paris—ABC Television Networks, Sherry Eaker—Backstage Publications, Lillian LaSalle—LaSalleHolland, The Actor's Federal Credit Union, Stephanie Berry, Willa Belle Marcellas, Zenobia Conkerite, Dr. Linda Morrison Combs, DC Walton, Greg Amerson, Phyllis Van Pelt, Greg Balkco, Jimmy Barden, K. Callons, Gwen Feldman, Jeffrey Black, Jon Lezinsky, Scott Hull—Scott Hull & Associates, Dr. Greg Ruvolo—Sound Body & Soul, Dr Jason Piken—Innate Chiropractic, Francisco-Mark Albert Hair Design, NYC, and Dr. Thomas Romo—Little Baby Face Foundation.

All my love and deep gratitude for all time to my Amazing and Unforgettable Mother: Mae Baker, and my Magnificent and Wonderful brothers: Kevin, Michael, and Stanley Baker.

Also to my Loving and Supportive surrounding families: Kelli, Molly, Sean, Maya, Solange & Rhone Baker. Ngozi, Eva, Elaine, Ricky, Kim & Tyler Gaskins.

My outstanding teachers from my Self-Expression and Leadership courses at Landmark Education, 2003-2004: the Marvelous Carla Satoff; the Effervescent Donna Eller; and my Spectacular Coach, Barbara Storey.

A special thank you to my One-of-a-Kind Literary Agent, Sharlene Martin of Martin Literary Management; my Fearless Publisher, Connie Shaw of Sentient Publications; my Immense Cheerleader, Lynne Carey of The Alzheimer's Association; and my Exceptional Editor with the Midas touch, Linda Nathan of Logos Word Designs, Inc.

Contents

Foreword

I HAVE BEEN ASKED TO WRITE MANY FOREWORDS, PARTICULARLY FOR BOOKS related in some way to Alzheimer's disease, but I've always declined, mainly because I didn't have time to read all those books and writing a foreword to a book I hadn't read seemed, well, backward.

But *Secrets of Voice-Over Success* just grabbed me. It grabbed me because I have both a love of its subject—the art of the voice-over, and a passion for its mission—the fight against Alzheimer's.

My love of voice-over developed doing animated films like *A Bug's Life, Treasure Planet,* and *Osmosis Jones,* narrating documentaries, recording books on tape, and doing radio commercials and voices for feature films.

My passion for fighting Alzheimer's came from losing friends and family, including my grandfather and my dad, to this terrible disease. And my passion is fueled by the dedication, generosity, and inspiration of my friends and colleagues at the Alzheimer's Association.

Dedication, generosity, and inspiration seem to be the underlying themes of this book. The artists writing here each talk about how important those qualities are for a successful voice-over career. And in sharing their insights, advice, successes, and failures, they demonstrate that generosity and dedication, inspiring the rest of us who toil (or hope to toil) in the voice-over business.

Perhaps the most important message of *Secrets of Voice-Over Success* is this: You are not alone. You are not alone in the sense that a successful voice-over career depends on agents and producers and mixers and clients and on and on. But, also, you are not alone in your struggles and successes and failures and hopes and dreams-the artists in this book have been where you are, and somewhere in their stories you will recognize your own.

That is also the message of the Alzheimer's Association. Alzheimer's is a terribly isolating disease, and the most important mission of the Association is to show Alzheimer's sufferers and their families that they are not alone.

So although this is supposed to be a foreword, it's really just a thank-you note. Thanks to Joan Baker for creating this great project, and to all the voice-over artists who so generously gave their time and shared their lives and to those of you buying this book, thank you all for lending your voices to the millions who suffer from Alzheimer's and for reminding them that they are not alone.

David Hyde Pierce

Introduction

SECRETS OF VOICE-OVER SUCCESS IS A CELEBRATION OF THE RARE FEW performers whose individual journeys may differ, but whose passion and commitment have led them to impeccable careers. The profession of voice-over artist is comprised of different kinds of performers, with different kinds of backgrounds and personalities, who have a voice that is special. Successful voice-over artists are the most famous, anonymous people in the country. They are employed by motion picture studios to sell movies, animation studios to create characters, advertising agencies to sell products, political consultants to create politicians' images, corporations to narrate corporate communications, documentary filmmakers to tell their stories, television networks to promote programming, radio conglomerates to promote radio stations and voice radio shows, and publishers to bring to life recorded books.

The voice business is a niche business. Of the many thousands of people who will try to pursue the riches of a career in this enigmatic and sometimes elusive corner of the entertainment industry, only a small minority will ever succeed. Every single voice-over performer who sustains a livelihood in this business, despite the insane odds against it, must do so with passion and commitment and each must be driven by an internal voice that beckons, despite the likelihood of failure, to keep going, keep trying. To describe the love of the voice-over business, one must first imagine something most people cannot imagine: spending most of your days in the auditioning process pursuing many jobs you will probably never win. Few if any of those jobs will pay guaranteed income. It is a daily roll of the dice, a bona fide chase to land work that may never pay off. That is the job. The successful voice-over career is born from a love of performing, and it is built upon equal parts talent, tenacity, and the love of winning, but it can be as infuriating and dismal as it can be uplifting and rewarding. It is in those ups and downs that the performer discovers the raison d'etre of this chosen profession. This work is a calling.

Very few people outside this business have ever stood behind the glass in a recording booth, hearing their own disembodied voice feed back through their headphones, working at the mercy of a talk-back mike, waiting for a producer to critique what they have read, sometimes hearing the conversation on the other side of the glass and sometimes not, waiting until they are given the cue and then being asked to read again maybe even fifty times until the producer feels it is just the right read. This process might take hours and may seem perplexing, but I have learned to understand it.

Not unlike many of my clients, I suppose I could have done easier things with my life, but for me, too, this was a calling. I came to New York from New England to study acting. I knew from the time I was very young that I would work in the entertainment industry and I was determined to fulfill my own calling. In retrospect, my entry into my now chosen profession seems like divine intervention. I was attending a lecture. Behind me sat a much older white haired man with a beret who asked me if I wanted to meet Tom Wolfe, his client, who was lecturing. I was curious enough. It didn't take long for him to figure out that I was then recently out of work, and his desire for an attractive assistant was stronger than his need for someone who could type. I figured out that unemployment was not going to afford me the lifestyle I believed I deserved. His name was Lester Lewis, and he was, although somewhat infamous, one of the first commercial agents. He did teach me a thing or two even if I had to put up with his cigar smoking and his inappropriate behavior in and out of the office. Over the next few months of my enduring his "guidance" and no less than a major blowout between us every day, he finally gave me the opportunity to help cast a new animated series. We landed three of the six parts in *Thundercats*. That experience catapulted me into the voice business and my own pursuit of working for a bigger agency.

Today, with twenty years of experience as an agent, it has been an amazing journey for me. I love my work and I consider it a privilege to have both represented and befriended some of the industry's most prominent and successful voice performers.

I am often asked how I go about picking the winners, how I identify a developmental performer that will make it. It is a good question. But it's like asking a painter how they paint. I do not know. I know how I listen to presentation material, I know how to listen to a voice, I know if there is good work going on in the interpretation of copy, I know a well made demo from a poorly made one and how to audition a potential client; how to direct, work, and extract the reads, pulling and shaping from those initial choices that won't cut it to those that will make the spot. And perhaps, most importantly, I know how to market a voice. I know how to create and nurture relationships with my clients and buyers that have lasted for decades. There has to be an organic "catch"—a chemistry that feels right. It is a dance. It has to do with intuition and belief and a feeling I get that this someone will be someone special in the business. Only exceptional performers work consistently. It is often a long process built from hard work in the studio, hours of coaching and reading and training the voice and the ear, and hours of figuring out who this person is and who they are not; what their attitude is toward themselves, the business, other performers; how they handle the pressure and take criticism; and how much they can take of this very difficult day to day life they are choosing. This is not a hobby for me or for my clients; it is not a part time job. It is a test of emotional stamina and commitment. We are a team, and together we succeed or fail.

I will never know the loneliness of the pursuit. I will never live the endless running around, the frustrations of daily rejection, the elation of a first booking that could change my life. I listen to the stories daily. I have compassion. But mostly, I work in the background, creating the opportunities, solving the problems, negotiating the deals. Day after day the driving force behind my work is the love, and the belief, that somehow what I bring to this will make a difference in the lives of the performers I represent.

They supply the talent, the spirit, the mindfulness, and the determination that will make them a success, and together we answer to the calling.

Robin Stecher
Executive Vice President
Don Buchwald and Associates

Preface

SECRETS OF VOICE-OVER SUCCESS IS AN INSPIRATIONAL, REAL-WORLD, practical handbook for anyone seeking a career in the sometimes but not always lucrative field of voice-over acting. Through the compelling stories of nineteen highly successful voice-over professionals, *Secrets of Voice-Over Success* teaches novices and acting professionals everything they'll need, from developing their talent to landing that first big job. And unlike other books that have attempted to uncover the mysteries of the voice-over industry, *Secrets of Voice-Over Success* provides a stunningly comprehensive picture by a rare and remarkably unselfish group sharing not only the tricks and secrets of the trade but, more importantly, their journeys to success.

Each story is guided by a uniquely developed series of penetrating questions born out of the experience of seasoned voice-over artists, agents, and producers speaking to the practical guidelines as well as to the emotional poise required to succeed in the voice-over industry. These are the topics they cover:

- The art and technique of voice-over
- The demo tape
- Obtaining and partnering with an agent
- Finding work

- The audition process
- Understanding and overcoming your fears and obstacles
- Keeping yourself motivated and inspired
- The business of being your own business
- Career development and networking
- Growing your skills—the never-ending pursuit of excellence

The power of providing how-to information through a unique variety of multi-faceted personal stories is that it reveals the humanity, pursuit, and breadth behind what might otherwise be mere technical information and empty career strategies. *Secrets of Voice-Over Success* is meant to inspire readers by showing them the human struggle involved in building a career and giving numerous examples of the strength and courage it takes to overcome one's personal attitudes and occupational obstacles. The book conveys these skills through a comprehensive and holistic perspective that cuts across gender, race, and age. One or two points of view are simply not enough for anyone to fully understand what it means to learn the craft of voice-over and launch a career. The goal of *Secrets of Voice-Over Success* is to facilitate your voice-over path by fully exposing and embracing the emotional side of building a rewarding career.

The Genesis of Voice-Over

IN A BOOK FEATURING MANY OF THE GREAT VOICE-OVER PERFORMERS OF OUR day, it's fair to ask, just what is a voice-over? The dictionary says, "In motion pictures and television, the voice of a narrator who does not appear on camera." But there's more to it than that. Voice-overs can be *any* announcement heard along with (or over) another medium. This expands the meaning from radio, film, and television to theater, telecommunications, video games, handheld computers, and so forth. A voice spoken while watching a visual or even while listening to another sound can be a voice-over, too. The railroad conductor calling "All aboard," the town crier shouting "Hear ye, hear ye," and even Congressional Doorkeeper William "Fishbait" Miller intoning, "The President of the United States" were all voice-over announcers.

Ancient Echoes

He ceased: but left so charming on their ear His voice, that listening still they seemed to hear.

—Homer in *The Odyssey*

The Greeks had a word for it, and it was *Coryphaeus* (kor-ee-phay-us). As the tradition of the theatre and a performance evolved out of pre-history, the now legendary name of *Thespis* is credited with creating the first dramatic play about 534 B.C. The performances took place in the Theatre of Dionysus on the Acropolis in Athens. These shows were held outdoors, the players used costumes and masks, and there were only three actors, no matter how many characters were in the play (obviously, non-union shop). A male chorus of twelve to fifteen commented on the characters and situations in the play and was led by the Coryphaeus, or choral leader. It was his voice only that interacted with the performers. He was the intermediary between the chorus, which represented the voice of the people, and the performers, who spoke the thoughts of the playwright. For example, in *Agamemnon*, a drama by Aeschylus, we hear:

Chorus: "I am come, reverencing power in thee, O Klutaimnestra, for 'tis just we bow to the ruler's wife."

Klutaimnestra: "Good news announcer, may as is the by-word Morn become truly, news from Night, his Mother."

The use of this "voice-over" commentator would become more or less popular, changing with the traditions of theatre over the centuries. A thousand years after Aeschylus, the voice-over was still heard in the English morality play *Everyman*. This box-office hit (it is still being performed occasionally today) of the fifteenth century changed the Coryphaeus to a messenger (representing Beauty). The play begins:

Messenger: "I pray you all give your audience, and hear this matter with reverence. By figure a moral play, the Summoning of Everyman called it is."

The plays of Shakespeare, the works of Eugene O'Neill and Bertolt Brecht, the use of the aside directly to the audience, the off-stage narrator, and even George Burns standing at the side of the stage holding an unlit cigar and commenting on the antics of Gracie all carry on the tradition of the voice-over in theatre. A fondly remembered re-appearance of the Coryphaeus came to American audiences from 1850 to 1870 in the form of the minstrel show and its interlocutor. As vaudeville and burlesque flourished until the invention of film and radio, the term changed to *host* or *master of ceremonies*. The announcers until this time all had at least one thing in common: None of them needed electricity to do a voice-over.

The Electric Announcer

The voice is nothing but beaten air. (*Vox nihil aliud quam ictus aer*).

- Seneca

Voice over a wire (the telephone) and voice over wax and shellac (recordings) both had their tentative beginnings about 1877. Thomas Edison designed and had built a recording phonograph and made the first announcement into it, reciting, "Mary Had A Little Lamb." The tinfoil used by Edison to record these words was replaced with a cylinder of more practical brown wax, then an improved black wax, and eventually a secret material called Amberol. One of Edison's assistants at the factory in New Jersey (actually the world's first research laboratory) recalled the boss pouring in the unidentified Amberol powder from a paper bag. Mr. Edison didn't consider his invention as a means of entertainment (a self-fulfilling prophecy in today's record market), but as a business device to be used for dictation. Emil Berliner's development of the flat disc in 1887 and an easy means to mass-produce the records brought out Edison's competitive spirit. Berliner's discs had only one side recorded; the double-faced record hadn't yet been offered. Edison realized the potential to use recordings for entertainment in the home and began recording music cylinders with famous opera singers, instrumentalists, marching bands, vocalists, duets, and dance orchestras. He chose who would and would not make Edison cylinders and, like record producers today, had a unique concept of what was good or bad. He was very hard of hearing, which would be a definite plus in today's record industry. If Thomas Edison liked your act, and you had the lung power to sing the same tune over and over again into the spring-wound recording machines, you were in.

The early Berliner discs had the name of the song and performer etched onto the disc itself. Paper record labels were an idea for the future. Edison's cylinders were about the size and shape of the cardboard core of a roll of toilet paper, but with a slightly larger diameter. The cylinders had no room on them to indicate the song title and performer. This information was printed on the lid of the box in which the cylinder was sold and on a slip of paper placed within the cylinder. This system worked until you played more than one tune during the evening, after which a problem arose as to which cylinder belonged in which box. And so, to help cure this problem of identification (according to one theory), the first announcer on phonograph records was born. Edison wanted a strong voice (the preferred adjective was *stentorian*) to introduce the music thusly: "*Across the Bridge of Gold*, sung by Byron G. Harlan, Edison Records." The word *Edisonnnnn* was drawn out in a unique style so the voice became recognizable from all others. This announcement made pirating the cylinders (a problem even then) more difficult because you couldn't edit out the announcement identifying the recording as an Edison product. Just to make sure, each box holding an Edison cylinder bore his autograph and the slogan, "None genuine without this signature."

One of the best remembered of these announcers was Edward Meeker, who also sang for the Edison label and even did maintenance at the West Orange studio as well (the world's first combo-man?). Arthur Collins was another Edison announcer (when he wasn't singing duets with Mr. Byron G. Harlan). Len Spencer was an announcer for the competing Columbia brand of cylinders. Mr. Berliner and his flat discs needed no announcer. The practice of cylinder announcements began about 1892 and continued until about 1912 when Edison introduced his molded Amberol records. These did have room to emboss the name of the tune and performer directly on the end of the cylinder.

One of Mr. Edison's many other inventions was a perfected motion picture camera in 1899. His success with this device was due, in no small part, to the invention of a celluloid film by George Eastman. Edison's Vitascope had publicly been introduced at a vaudeville show on April 23, 1896, but it was considered a mere novelty. His eventual success with shooting movies and projecting them led to an attempt to combine this visual process with his phonograph and make sound movies. Edison's

Kinetophone or Kinetophonograph was not a success because of the inability to synchronize the sound from the cylinder record with the film being projected.

The first film voice-over had to wait for one more necessary invention. At almost the same time Edison invented the phonograph, Alexander Graham Bell perfected his telephone, making voice-over-a-wire possible. The first message spoken on this startling new invention was the often quoted, "Watson, come here, I need you." Thomas Watson (Bell's assistant, not the friend of Sherlock Holmes) thus received the first telephone message, a distress call, decades before 911. Almost as soon as home telephones were installed, telephone wires were used to transmit entertainment and news announcements. Live music by telephone was heard at the 1881 Paris International Electrical Exhibition. Two telephone lines were used for stereo reception, which was referred to as binauriclar audition. Coin operated receivers called The Theatrephone were offered in 1890, and Telefon Hirmondo became well known in Hungary for presenting the news by telephone. Who read this news? Who introduced this music?

One amusing idea began in Connecticut in 1894, when Time By Telephone began to offer continuous time signals to subscribers. If you didn't pay, an attachment called the confuser would scramble the signal! I wouldn't be surprised if somebody had built the first cheater-box in 1895! Washington, Indiana offered church services by telephone in 1902. The Tellevent was announced in 1907 to "supply subscribers at their homes with the latest happenings of the world, with special music, performances at theatre, concerts and churches." A Telephone Announcement Service offered "weather forecasts, market reports and the correct time . . . along with commercial announcements." The year 1909 saw the start of Tel-Musici of Delaware, a pay-per-play service, and the world's first all-request show.

A rare combination of a spark gap transmitter and a microphone (the carbon-granule packed mouthpiece of a telephone) was achieved by Reginald Fessenden, a British scientist, on Christmas Eve, 1906. In a transmission to those few ships at sea that had radios (it was not a requirement to have a radio on board a passenger ship until after the *Titanic* sank in 1912), Fessenden became one of the first known persons to speak on radio.

He introduced a female acquaintance who sang a few Christmas carols, followed by Mr. Fessenden himself playing the violin.

Two years later, Lee De Forest, a master of self-aggrandizement, began a series of *broadcasts* (a newly coined term) from atop the Eiffel tower. He was heard five hundred miles away in Marseilles by the use of what must have been a remarkable transmitter site. In 1910, Mr. De Forest broadcast Enrico Caruso singing from the stage of the Metropolitan Opera in New York City. Who would have been listening? Amateur radio enthusiasts and experimenters only. If you wanted a radio, you had to build one; there were none for sale. In a famous memo, the young telegrapher who received the transmissions from the ship *Carpathia* with survivor lists from the *Titanic* proposed that a radio music box be placed in every home. The 1916 note to his boss at the Marconi Company suggested that the company provide a series of programs for those with these devices to hear. The telegrapher's name was David Sarnoff (the future president of RCA and NBC), and for the time being his advice was ignored.

Wireless Telephony

I introduced the Duchess of Dundee
Over the facilities of WABC,
Her organs internal
Made noises infernal
And everyone thought it was me.
                              —Anonymous

By the summer of 1920, several organizations were preparing to go on the air as a form of entertainment and education. Up to this point, the main purpose of radio was communication (i.e., wireless telegraphy and wireless telephony). Why would anyone want to start a radio station? It was certainly not to make money. The licenses were almost free. Jack Poppele, the man who put WOR on the air (and its chief engineer for many years), recalled that he took the train down to the Department of Commerce in Washington, D. C. He paid the small fee, filled out the forms, and returned to New York with permission to begin broadcasting for Bamberger's department store in Newark. There weren't many people listening; in fact you still couldn't buy an assembled radio (even at Bamberger's). Among the first assembled receiving sets for the home was one that was introduced by Powel Crosley, Jr. in 1921. It sold for $35. Those made by Mr. Atwater Kent in 1922 were much more expensive, and the concept of a step-up model was born. After you purchased a radio, you still had to acquire the options of three different size batteries, an aerial, a speaker or a pair of headphones, and a complete set of vacuum tubes. This was an early use of the concept "Accessories sold separately."

Who was the first radio announcer? It all depends on what you mean by first. Was it the first person whose voice was ever broadcast? Was it the first person to speak on the first radio station? How about the first person who was ever paid for speaking on the air or who regularly announced as a profession? Let's tune in on that fateful election eve in 1920. KDKA had received its license only a week earlier. Frank Conrad, the assistant chief engineer for Westinghouse, had been on the air as early as 1916 as an amateur, using the call letters 8XK. This first station with all letters (no numbers) in its call sign (a relatively new term) was located in a shack on the ninth floor roof of a building housing the Westinghouse advertising department. Mr. Conrad was at his home, ready to go on the air with his own equipment just in case the KDKA transmitter didn't work. There were four men in the studio that evening. One man wrote down the election returns read over the telephone from the *Pittsburgh Post*. A second man represented the telephone company who had installed the temporary phone lines. A third man operated the transmitter (they needed attention as transmitters at this time tended to blow the final output tubes when over-modulated, and I do mean blow). The fourth man was twenty-four-year-old Leo Rosenberg. Leo worked at the advertising department of Westinghouse and was the first man to speak on the new station (I guess making Rosenberg the first ethnic broadcaster as well). For the first time, we had a record of exactly what was said on one of these historic occasions. He said, "This is station K-D-K-A, Westinghouse, East Pittsburgh, Pennsylvania." Of course, no recording was made of this pedestrian announcement, but in 1941, on the station's twenty-first anniversary, this exact scene was re-enacted by those who were there and by those who listened in. It is this 1941 recording recreating the first broadcast that gives us a sound picture of the first radio program. The letters K-D-K-A were said slowly and clearly, as reception was often filled with static. The station transmitted at 360 meters (a frequency of about 830 kilocycles). The number of listeners this evening not connected with the Westinghouse Company was probably very small. Of course there were no ratings that night. In fact, there were still no radios for sale. (The term *radio* wasn't well known, it was still *wireless* to most people.)

KDKA continued the next night with a regular but brief schedule. Leo Rosenberg announced each evening from 8:00 to 9:30 or 10:00 p.m. in addition to his regular job in the advertising department. As Christmas 1920 approached, Rosenberg felt he had had enough of radio and auditioned a young electrical engineer from Kansas who was taking a Westinghouse graduate student training course. The engineer's name was Harold Arlin. He possessed a voice that was "vigorous and carried well," a requirement similar to Ed Meeker's qualifications on Edison's cylinders. It was almost December 21 when Arlin was offered the job as the world's first full time radio announcer. His reply to this opportunity for immortality was, "Yeah."

The first radio announcer in the New York area was hired by WJZ in Newark. Westinghouse duplicated the KDKA studio and transmitter atop their New Jersey factory building and hired "Tommy" Cowan as the full-time announcer. His first words, during a September, 1921, broadcast were, "This is WJZ, WJZ, WJZ, the radio telephone station located in Newark, New Jersey. This is announcer Cowan, Newark." You can tell that the idea of "furniture that talks" (a quip made years later by Fred Allen) was still a novel one. The programming didn't much matter; what was exciting about this cutting edge technology was that it actually spoke to you! Tommy Cowan often referred to himself on the air as "ACN," starting a long tradition of announcers using only initials or their last names.

The number of announcers multiplied as fast as the many stations that began transmissions in the next few years. There were literally hundreds of famous announcers starting at this time. A few names you might remember are: H. V. Kaltenborn, Ben Grauer, Ted Husing, Milton Cross, Graham McNamee, Floyd Gibbons, George Hay (creator of *The Grand Ole Opry*), and Bill Hay (who introduced *Amos 'n' Andy* for over twenty years). In 1924, WJZ ran a want ad in *The New York Times*. "Wanted: Announcer for metropolitan radio station. Must be college graduate and have knowledge of music terminology. Apply Broadcast Central, 33 West 42nd Street, New York City." Norman Brokenshire, who became one of radio's best-known announcers, got the job. He later modestly admitted, "For those crude mikes, my voice was perfect. I could vary the tone, the speed, the expression; the engineer's control needle would scarcely waver."

WEAF in New York City introduced a new concept in broadcasting in 1922. The station was owned by AT&T, which was then *the* telephone company, and its idea was to sell time on the station to those willing to pay for it. This was to be similar to a toll call on the telephone and was even referred to as toll broadcasting. The very first commercial came on the air at 5:15 p.m., August 28, 1922. The product? A real estate development in Queens, New York. A talk was given not by a professional announcer, but by a Mr. Blackwell of the Queensboro Corporation. The copy was written by Griffin Radio Service, Inc., an advertising agency that used a style far different from what we've come to know. A brief excerpt follows (read slowly and with feeling):

> I wish to thank those within the sound of my voice for the broadcasting opportunity afforded me to urge this vast radio audience to seek the recreation and the daily comfort of the home removed from the congested part of the city, right at the boundaries of God's great outdoors, and within a few minutes by subway from the business section of Manhattan. The cry of the heart is for more living room, more chance to unfold, and more opportunity to get near to Mother Earth, to play, to romp, to plant, and to dig. Let me enjoin upon you as you value your health and your hopes and your happiness, get away from the solid masses of brick, where the meager opening admitting a slant of sunlight is mockingly called a light shaft, and where children grow up starved for a run over a patch of grass and the sight of a tree.

This went on for another fifteen minutes. Commercial broadcasting was a great opportunity for the professional announcer, when the agency did not yield to the temptation to allow the sponsor to speak for himself. And while announcing a sponsored program was more lucrative than doing one without a sponsor (referred to as *sustaining*), sponsoring a radio show became an effort to be commercial without being crass. One way of achieving this was to name the performer after the product. The late 1920s featured programs such as *The Atwater Kent Hour, The Eveready Hour, The A & P Gypsies, Enna Jettick Melodies, The Studebaker Champions, Soconyland Sketches, The Pure Oil Band, The Dutch Master Minstrels* and the enigmatically named *Prophylactic Program.* (Relax, it was the Victor Arden Orchestra and a male trio.) This association of the program name or the performers with the sponsor was considered enough advertising on most programs. A dignified announcement that, "The preceding broadcast of *The Palmolive Hour* was brought to you by the makers of Palmolive Soap, Cincinnati, Ohio" was deemed sufficient.

The Voice from the Screen

A word fitly spoken is like apples of gold in pictures of silver.
—Proverbs 25:11 (KJV).

While radio was finding its voice during the early 1920s, so too was film. A 1923 invention by Lee De Forest started to make sound films practical. The synchronization process that bedeviled Edison was solved by what De Forest called the Phonophone System; it came to be known as Fox Movietone. Imprinting the sound track on the film itself using an optical system kept the images in synch with the sounds. Nothing seems more disconcerting to audiences than improper lip-synch.

Even though 1927 audiences were much less sophisticated about sound than we are today, the sound-on-film methods were obviously superior, and even Warner Brothers eventually abandoned the sound-on-disc method. The following year, the first all-talking feature was released. It was a gangster movie called *The Lights of New York.* During one of the scenes, one killer is shown holding a gun on his victim. Turning to his henchman, the first bad guy says for the first time that now famous line of dialogue (read slowly and with menace), "Take him for a ride."

A valuable byproduct of this failed synchronization method was the sixteen-inch electrical transcription that was adopted by the radio industry and made pre-recorded radio programs practical. These programs were not sent to individual stations on network wires but were transcribed and sent by mail or Railway Express. This syndication of canned programming opened yet another new field requiring the services of announcers. Programs were either recorded just for syndication or, later, recorded off a network line on instantaneous acetates for local rebroadcast. This method of distribution was used in 1928 for the first time by Freeman Gosden and Charles Correll. They successfully distributed 78 rpm records of their *Amos 'n' Andy* show to stations beyond WMAQ in Chicago.

The year 1928 also saw the first animated talking film, a natural opportunity for voice-over announcers, as all animated films are. *Steamboat Willie* featured a singing and whistling mouse with the voice-over by a cartoonist from Kansas City named Walt Disney. The art form of the newsreel required voice-over announcers as well. Newsreels were started in Europe as a weekly feature by Pathe in 1907. By the 1920s, International Newsreel, Metrotone, Hearst, and Fox Movietone newsreels were seen across the country. When most theatres had converted to talkies, the newsreels added stirring music, sound effects, and voice-over narration to what was silent footage. Lowell Thomas, Ed Herlihy, and Westbrook Van Voorhis (known as "The Voice Of Doom" for his pronouncements on *The March Of Time*) became well known. Sound footage was gradually added during the early 1930s until the idea of the newsreel died in the early '60s (its death partially attributed to *The Huntley-Brinkley Report*).

Travelogues were usually scenic-but-silent footage with voice-over narration. This was a time in film history when people went to the movies several times a week. Double features were common, as were assorted short subjects, a newsreel, and a cartoon (several cartoons and forget the newsreel if it was a Saturday matinee). This was a wonderful time to be a voice-over announcer. Dozens of companies, large and small, were producing one- and two-reelers, cartoons, even educational, religious, and sponsored films. Now that films spoke, the dialogue had to be re-dubbed before exporting the movie to a non-English speaking country, and so yet another sub-industry for voice-overs was born. Feature films seldom used voice-over narrators (Billy Wilder being a notable exception with *Double Indemnity*, *Hollywood Boulevard* and *The Seven Year Itch*). However, almost all features of note required a voice-over for the Coming Attractions. One of the characters on the Fred Allen radio show (Minerva Pious as Mrs. Nussbaum) once complained, "Always next week is coming a good picture." Using stirring music, excerpts from the film, and an exuberant voice-over announcer, the movie trailer promoting not-yet-released films ("Coming to this theatre, Thursday") made even the worst turkey sound pretty good.

Radio and Radio with Pictures

> I used to sit with Mary when the family went to bed,
> But now she has a radio and all her love is 'dead,'
> The family simply 'sticks' around 'til one o'clock or two,
> I cannot spoon with Mary now; pray tell me what to do.
> —*Radio Age Weekly*, issue of November 28, 1925

It will come as no surprise that radio gained in popularity as the Depression continued into the Roosevelt administration. Once you owned a radio set, the evening's entertainment was free and plentiful. Chain broadcasting began in 1926 with the formation of NBC and its two networks (the Red and the Blue). The Columbia Phonograph Company took over the foundering United Broadcasters Inc. on September 18, 1927 and became The Columbia Phonograph Broadcasting Company, which became The Columbia Broadcasting System in January 1929. The major investor in the new company was William Paley, heir to a family fortune acquired from the manufacture of cigars. The slogan of their best-remembered brand was "La Palina cigars contain no spit!" As catchy as this slogan might have been, it was discontinued when it was revealed that La Palinas were indeed made with spit.

In addition to these national chains, there were many regional networks (The Don Lee Network, The Colonial Network, The Yankee Network, and The RKO Network) and hundreds of independent stations. Each new network required announcers, newscasters, sportscasters, cooking and home-making experts, music specialists, and, of course, commercial spokesmen.

As the 1930s continued, many announcers became celebrities in themselves. Harry Von Zell not only sold Sal Hepatica on *The Fred Allen Show*, but he also became a comic foil for Eddie Cantor. You seldom heard Bing Crosby without the mellow voice and Kraft commercials of Ken Carpenter. Harlow Wilcox became known as "Waxy" for the clever way the

Johnson's Wax commercials were integrated into *Fibber McGee and Molly*. What would a Jell-O commercial on *The Jack Benny Show* sound like without the enthusiastic voice of Don Wilson reciting those six delicious flavors? Some, just some, of those famous voices of the period were: Howard Petrie, Ken Niles, Jim Ameche, Graham McNamee, Ford Bond, Ken Roberts, Alois Havrilla, Bud Collyer, Dan Seymour, Frank Singiser, Marvin Miller, Mike Wallace (still known as "Myron Wallace"), Mel Allen, Louis A. Witten, Andre Baruch, Basil Ruysdael, and hundreds more. Starting as announcers only, many well known radio voices found themselves starring in programs of their own. Jim Ameche became Jack Armstrong. In 1940, Bud Collyer went from being the announcer on *The Cavalcade of America* to the dual role of Superman and Clark Kent.

During the Second World War, which began for Europe in September 1939, the announcer took on a newly expanded role, that of newscaster. CBS had the advantage of already having Edward R. Murrow in London when hostilities began. His title was European Director of Talks, and his job before the war was to schedule programs like the Vienna Boys Choir, political talks, and discussion programs. When the war started, he hired journalists to report from the foreign capitals, and suddenly *The World News Roundup* (that began the year before) took on a new importance. For the first time, the situations in nations at war could be heard directly from the scene. Murrow's boys, as they would come to be known, were chosen for their reporting ability rather than the quality of their voices. They would soon become household names: William L. Shirer, Eric Sevareid, Winston Burdett, Charles Collingwood, Ned Calmer, Richard C. Hottelet, and Howard K. Smith. NBC and Mutual both used print journalists and European broadcasters who were already overseas to cover the news. NBC's strength lay in the quality of its analysis, commentary, and domestic reporting, with voices like Lowell Thomas, Morgan Beatty, H. R. Baukhage, Upton Close, Merrill Mueller, Richard Harkness, and later H. V. Kaltenborn.

Reporting the news required a voice with believability, calm (even when you were on a London roof while bombs were falling), the ability to write for the ear (as opposed to "rip and read" from the teletypes intended for newspapers), and the ability to pronounce far away places with strange sounding names. Even as suave an announcer as CBS's John Daly was at a loss on how to pronounce *Oahu* on a December Sunday in 1941. An unusual type of voice-over announcing was made popular by none other than Adolf Hitler, who spoke only in German on the air. During Hitler's broadcast speeches, NBC's bilingual announcer Max Jordan would interrupt the talk in progress (they went on for some time) for a summary of the last few paragraphs and a recap after the end. A new form of voice-over developed and was a marked improvement; it was called simultaneous English. The announcer would speak *over* the lowered voice of Mr. Hitler and translate the words as they were spoken. As you can imagine, this was not easy to do, even with an advance text of the address, which announcers were seldom given. This form of literal voice-over was perfected and continues today on live television and at the United Nations, where simultaneous translations are common. Incidentally, the United Nations used to have its own radio service, but it declined its own FM frequency in New York City when it was offered one at no charge by the United States. This took place in 1945—who was going to listen to something called "FM"?

Shortly after the war, broadcasting began to change. At the 1939 World's Fair, President Roosevelt spoke at the RCA exhibit and was seen by the newly improved television camera. How many people saw that early TV broadcast? Probably fewer than heard the election returns on KDKA in 1920. Why would anyone want a television set? Very few had been sold by RCA, and those were ridiculously expensive. The fact that there were no programs on the air also might have discouraged sales; it was a typical chicken-and-egg situation. The research and development of television had been halted by the war, but it continued soon after V-J Day. Television transmissions were mostly local and were available in very few cities. A TV network could mean as few as two stations, and coast-to-coast live television was still several years away. Network television required something called a co-axial cable, of which there were few. Those few network TV shows in 1946 included such gems as *I Love To Eat, The Gillette Cavalcade of Sports, Western Movie,* and *Let's Rhumba.* NBC and DuMont were the only networks with announced programs. On Mondays, NBC started its schedule at 7:45 PM with *Esso Newsreel.* There were no daytime shows; there were no programs at all on Saturday.

Despite this tentative beginning, television did grow rapidly, creating more announcing and voice-over opportunities. You soon could see for yourself that Don Wilson really was fat (he and Jack Benny were now selling Lucky Strikes). Ed Herlihy had a double chin from munching on Kraft Macaroni and Cheese and Velveeta. George Fenneman was handsome and sophisticated, which made people want to smoke the Chesterfields he was selling. And few could resist Durward Kirby assuring them that, "If I liked peanuts, I'll *love* Skippy!" Bill Shipley's pompadour was perfect to assure guys of a smooth shave with Schick razors and to try Old Spice afterward. Ernest Chappell told you that Pall Malls were "outstanding," while Cy Harrice confided, "And . . . they are mild!" Rex Marshall urged Mom to use Reynolds Wrap in the kitchen and touted the many benefits of "Putting a tiger in my tank." William Lundigan proudly displayed the tail-finned "New Look" of the Chrysler Corporation, while Betty Furness gracefully opened Westinghouse refrigerator doors. Miss Furness's failure to get the door open one night could have done little to help the cause of live commercials. Mike Wallace (no longer "Myron") sold Viceroys, and what was a baseball game without Mel Allen pouring a Ballantine on a hot summer's day by the set! How did he always get the beer to stop foaming just at the top of the glass? "Man, how 'bout that!"

The live announcers on television demonstrating the sponsor's product would soon disappear; they cost too much. A typical and very entertaining early example was Sid Stone, the sidewalk pitchman on Milton Berle's *Texaco Star Theatre.* "You say you're not satisfied, you say you want more for your money? Tell ya what I'm gonna do!" This entertaining commercial-comedy routine would be followed by four men in gas station uniforms singing, "O, we're the men from Texaco, We're known from Maine to Mexico . . ." This form of commercial-as-entertainment was not nearly as effective as drumming the same message or jingle into your head night after night. Commercials like ventriloquist Jimmy Nelson and his puppets Danny O'Day and Farfel ("N-E-S-T-L-E-S, Nestlé's makes the very best . . . chocolate!") gave way to an endlessly repeated cutaway drawing of the human stomach with the "A's" (Anacin) beating the "B's" (presumably Bufferin) into the bloodstream every time.

It was, therefore, the relatively anonymous voice-over announcer who became more wanted for filmed television commercials. These unseen voices were much cheaper than star-personality announcers on the screen, and what sponsor wouldn't rather see a close-up of the product than the smiling face of an announcer, hopefully holding the product right side up. On filmed commercials, celebrity announcers didn't become extinct. Orson Welles told viewers that Paul Masson "would sell no wine before its time." Laurence Olivier sold Polaroid cameras, and John Houseman assured us that Smith Barney would "make money the old fashioned way, by earning it!"

The human voice is the organ of the soul.

—Henry Wadsworth Longfellow

Don LaFontaine

Don LaFontaine is the voice of over 4,000 movie trailers and promotions and tens of thousands of promos for NBC, CBS, ABC, FOX, UPN, TNT, TBS, Spike TV, The Cartoon Network, and many others. He has been profiled on *Dateline*, CBS, CNN, and ABC. He is, arguably, the most successful voice-over artist of all time.

LUCK AND TIMING. THAT SUMS UP MY LIFE IN THE WORLD OF VOICE ACTING. I suppose my career track is unique in many ways. I know it certainly could never be duplicated. I started as a recording engineer, a trade I learned in the Army, and one thing led to another: writer, producer, director, and eventually voice actor. It all began for me in the early sixties, when the movie trailer business as we now know it was in its infancy. Prior to that time, trailers usually were cut by the editor of the feature film, sort of as an afterthought. These previews usually ran after the feature (hence the term *trailers*) and were finished in Hollywood at National Screen Service. Early trailers were pretty basic sales tools—hard sell, relying on hyperbole and star power to win an audience.

In the early sixties, some studios, like Metro-Goldwyn-Mayer and Columbia, began experimenting with going outside the system to create their sales tools. I was fortunate enough to be among the first group of outsiders to take a shot at it—maybe a dozen people in all, as opposed to the three dozen *companies* that exist today. As a fledgling writer, I didn't know there were rules to composing advertising copy, so I blithely went about breaking them, along with a few other people—Ed Apfel was the first among equals. He was a funereal young fellow, quiet and studious, and given to rolling a quarter over his knuckles as he created his mini-masterpieces of print copy or trailer narration. He was the best damn writer of that material that I've ever known. Floyd Peterson, who gave me my first break, was another. In January of 1963, he hired me away from National Recording Studios in Manhattan, and we became a two-man operation, cranking out radio spots for a rapidly growing clientele. We didn't know it at the time, but we were on the front lines of a revolution in advertising. The trailers and television promos you see today are the direct descendants of those early efforts.

I started doing voice-overs by accident. One night, I was in the midst of finishing no less than seven radio campaigns (all of which were due in the morning), and I had voice-over guys (then called announcers) lined up in the hallway outside the studio. One of them missed the booking, and because I had to present something to Columbia Pictures in the AM, I got behind the mike and recorded a scratch narration—something to indicate how the spot would sound if a real voice guy was on the project. The picture was *Gunfighters of Casa Grande*. Much to my amazement, Columbia bought the spots with my voice, and that was the beginning. It was a gradual process, but over the next few years I had the opportunity to voice dozens more projects.

Now, here's the unique part. My style evolved in a completely singular environment. First, we were dealing in a brand new art form—the modern trailer. Second, I was usually voicing material that I had written, so I knew exactly how it should sound, at least to me. Third, because I was giving myself the work, I was able to perform in many different genres: action, drama, comedy, romance, horror, science fiction . . . and consequently was able to find my voice in each of these areas. This simply does not happen these days. Most voice actors tend to be put into a specific box, and it's very difficult to get out of it.

For many years, I had the good fortune to be almost alone in the field. As a result, after forty-odd years in the game, most of the current crop of voice actors has grown up hearing me perform on a large number of the trailers and television spots for movies. It has left a sort of imprint on many of them, reflected in the way they deliver their lines. Don't get me wrong, I'm not saying that they're *imitating* me—it's just that the scripts have not changed all that much over the years, and there are time-tested ways to read them.

You couldn't get away with it today, but one thing I rarely did was to produce a demo reel. Since I specialized in a very specific field, everybody knew who I was, so the work just kept coming in. On one occasion, I did put together a compilation of a few spots and sent them to a major agency that handled announcers, with an eye to possibly breaking into the Madison Avenue commercial field. The tape was returned by the head of the agency, along with a brief note that advised me to forget it—I'd never have a career in voice-over. Luckily, I was too busy working in voice-over to take his advice.

Securing a talent agent to represent me was another career milestone that happened in an unorthodox manner. I had spent nearly twenty years in the business, but my primary job was as a producer of trailers, television spots, radio spots, and other sales tools for feature films. I had just finished a three-year stretch as VP of advertising at Paramount when I moved to Los Angeles, intending to continue working the same fields. One of the producers I had hired during my tenure at Paramount was named Larry Belling. He knew my voice work and he had been impressed. He told Steve Tisherman, his agent at the time, that I had moved from New York to Los Angeles. Shortly afterwards, the first phone call I received in my new apartment was from Steve. I really wasn't interested. After all, I had a steady stream of work without an agent, but he was persistent. Finally, mostly to get him off my back, I signed with him. It's been twenty-two years. He's still my agent.

Self-promotion is a necessary evil for today's voice-over artists, but I've never had to do it. I don't attempt to sell myself, for a very good reason. I'm rotten at it. Selling me is the job of my agent, and he's very good at it. My job is to show up on time, read the material to the client's satisfaction, sign my paperwork, and skedaddle.

A critical key to success in this game is how you impress your clients. Here are a few things I've learned over the years regarding my behavior vis-à-vis the people I work for: First, always be the same person—and that person should be polite, approachable, and helpful. Be that person every time. Your problems have no place in the studio. Being moody, impatient, and disrespectful—in short, acting like a star—will only make your job tougher. Remember, *you work for them.* Also keep in mind that if you're at all successful, on many occasions you're going to walk in, spend a short time reading aloud into a microphone, and then walk out—having just earned more money for that time period than everybody else in the room, *combined.* You could easily be resented for that, and these people not only control how you are going to sound on the finished product, they also have some control over any future employment. You do not want them as enemies.

You will often hear yourself referred to as the *talent.* Don't take it too seriously. In reality, you are usually only one part of the end product. If you're the talent, then what does that make the editor, the recording engineer, the producer, the director, the writer, the musicians? It's your job to make *their* job easier. Always be friendly and helpful but not overly humble or subservient. Remember, they're hiring you to be you. It helps if they truly *like* you.

Learn to self-edit. You will always know when your performance is less than your best. Always request another take if you're not satisfied—immediately. This will show the producer that you are giving him your best work and, more importantly, it will save you time in the long run, especially if you have an ongoing relationship with this client. Very quickly they will learn that when you want another take, there's a good reason for it. Conversely, when you *don't* request another take, you are tacitly approving the one you just finished. Over time, this approval will go a long way to convincing the producer that they have what they need. It will also make you the go-to person more often, because you save them time and effort.

Don't suck up! Please! Don't spend a lot of your time and money finding little gifts for your clients or sending thank-you notes after each session. I know this advice flies in the face of other opinions, but it's what has always worked for me. Think about it. You don't receive much more than a Christmas card from the people who work for you, like your mail carrier, your paper delivery boy, or your dry cleaner. There is no reason to be overtly grateful for the work. You're doing them as much of a favor by performing consistently as they are in giving you the job in the first place. It's a very symmetrical synergy.

I have been incredibly lucky with regard to overcoming any sort of major obstacle to my career. I have been pretty much bulletproof against serious problems. The only rough spots usually come from doing the job *too* well for an inexperienced or insecure producer. Here's the scenario: You nail the read on the first, second, or third take. The producer can't believe that you got it so quickly, so he or she asks for a few more protection takes. Now remember, the key to a successful voice-over is veracity—sounding spontaneous and sincere. The more takes you do, the more of that truth and spontaneity is leached out of the performance. What happens then is what I call The Slow, Agonizing Death of the Salesman. The hapless producer starts chasing what he or she heard in the first three takes but doesn't realize it, having already discounted those takes as too early to be good. So now there's an unconscious attempt to duplicate those early takes, usually by asking you to change the inflection on various words, and all the time taking you farther and farther away from what that person really wants. You, my friend, are now in voice-over hell. There really is no way out of it. Eventually, of course, the producer will give up and move on, but he or she might then carry the impression that working with you is like pulling teeth. It's one possible downside of being too good at what you do.

No matter how good you may be, you're not going to book every job for which you audition. Sometimes the answer is going to be no. I never let it bother me. I keep in mind that this is a very subjective business. I am certainly not right for every job. As an actor, rejection is the first thing with which you learn to deal. It's not so much rejection as it is a process of elimination. You do it all the time. If you select Burger King over McDonalds, you're not rejecting McDonalds; you simply prefer Burger King. That's the way it is in this business. Don't dwell on it. Move on. Believe me; your career is *not over*.

Keep your focus on bringing the copy to life. Copy tells me how it wants to be read. I look at the words. What is their mood? What is their message? Are the words happy or sad, angry or frightened, in love or in conflict? It's all in the words. I merely translate.

Here's the thing: We are all composites of our life experiences. That's what makes each one of us unique. I am the very best *me* in the world. Nobody else has lived the arc of my life. I alone carry my particular responses to what I feel and see—and that is reflected in how I read copy. How I feel fear impacts my interpretation of a horror script. My experiences with love come through in romantic copy, and so forth. There's no substitute for experience. The trick to letting those responses come through in your performance is—surprise!—practice.

And time. Lots of time.

The more you read and record, the more you will discover little tricks of phrasing and other methods of conveying the spirit of the script. Here's a small exercise: When you are about to read a piece of copy, you will feel it sort of swell up in your chest, just before you open your mouth. Try this: Ignore the first swell—and the second. Begin your read on the third and see how much better it is. I don't know why. I suppose it's just a matter of your system absorbing the material better prior to the performance. Try it. It works.

I can't give advice about finding work. Because of the way my career evolved, being on the ground floor of a new industry, work just finds me. Of course, my agent also negotiates additional projects, but I see those as extra trimmings. I (thank God) have never really needed to pursue work in this field. There are, of course, necessary elements to being competitive in the hunt: Get a good agent, have an impressive demo reel, and go out on as many auditions as humanly possible. You don't have to be *better* than the other guy, but you damn well have to be *as good*. Remember, most producers have already heard the voice they want in their heads. If you've got it, or if your performance is good enough to change their minds, you're in.

Aside from being heard by vast numbers of people, I still consider myself just another working stiff. Strangers *never* recognize my voice when I'm out in public. I don't use my performance voice(s) in public. If I did, they'd probably haul me off to a rubber room, somewhere. It's my voice—it's just *more*.

The other way that this work affects my daily life is that odd jobs show up from time to time. For example, I get asked to do a lot of answering machine messages for people. Occasionally I do a live event, and I'm always asked to emcee family functions. Outside of that, my work rarely impacts the other aspects of my life.

For people looking into the voice-over or entertainment business for the first time, a background in entertainment helps, but it is by no means necessary. A background in life, on the other hand, is indispensable. As I mentioned earlier, it is life experience that colors every reading. It is also not necessary to have a great speaking voice. A thunder throat is helpful only if you know how to use it. Simply being able to make glass vibrate by speaking does not assure you a place in the voice-over pantheon.

Forget your voice. It is what it is, and trying to change it will only make it sound false—unless, of course, you're going into animation work. Outside of that, there is a market for virtually *every voice*, as long as you make it work for you. How do you accomplish that? You could take a few courses. There are some reputable schools in the larger cities, but barring that, you could simply read. Read *everything* and *anything!* Read aloud into a recording device and play it back. Read familiar stuff like the Pledge of Allegiance or the inscription at the base of the Statue of Liberty, but read it like it really meant something. Give the words the respect and emotion they deserve. Do it right and you'll sometimes bring tears to your eyes. Read and listen. Try different inflections, speeds, and volumes. Over and over. Find *all* your voices. As I said earlier, most modern voice-over guys get put in a box and are limited in the range of work they can do. Don't make that mistake. If you have only one voice, fine. Perfect it and move on. If you can do more, do it! Make sure you're ready before you seek an agent or work. The old bromide about never getting a second chance to make a first impression is very true in this game.

Expect anonymity. Even though you're being heard by multitudes, you're not being *seen*. There is very little glory and public recognition in this business . . . but the money is good. As for me, I've always considered myself to be a behind-the-scenes sort of person. However, my longevity in this business and the need for print, radio, and television human-interest stories have brought me a measure of celebrity that I never expected. It's a little unsettling. It's also flattering. It's nice to know that you've made an impression, but, when all is said and done, the greatest joy comes from simply doing good work.

If I lost my voice, it would be devastating but not fatal. I would, out of necessity, adapt. I would find some other method of communication, but it wouldn't be the same. Your voice is a marvelous tool. Respect it. Train it. Use it well, and it can become the most powerful and productive muscle in your body.

1st SECRET

Vital to your success is how you conduct yourself with your clients. Your personal issues have no place in the studio.

Steve Zirnkilton

Steve Zirnkilton is the voice of NBC's *Law & Order* series. Other promo and narration credits include NBC, ABC, CNN, TLC, Discovery, TBS, MSNBC, and The Cartoon Network. His animated credits include *Rugrats: The Movie*, *Duckman*, and *Family Guy*. Baseball fans can hear him as the narrator for Major League Baseball's production, *Faith Rewarded: The Historic Season of The 2004 Boston Red Sox*.

BECOMING A WORKING VOICE TALENT REQUIRED A LOT OF PRACTICE AND advice from others in the industry and ultimately a little luck coupled with blind determination. A voice-over career has many twists and turns and is filled with emotional highs and lows. There are, however, fundamental differences between a day job and an acting or voice-over career. In this business, most people don't get a steady paycheck. As a result, we have some good years and some bad years. My wife and I worked long and hard to supplement our income with other jobs before we got to where we are now.

Alice Whitfield at Real to Reel Productions in New York produced my first real demo tape. Demos were longer back then, so I think we did something like eight spots. I arrived with a few years of experience in theater and radio from my college days. I also had done some work for a local television affiliate. Still, when you first start, it's easy to get uptight because you're on a tight budget, and time is money. Yet you also want to make the best possible production.

When my demo was finished, Alice sent it to an agent at one of the better agencies. He signed me immediately, and I booked my first job in no time: a radio spot for a mall in New Jersey. *Wow*, I thought, *this is easy*. I was wrong, very wrong. It took several more months before I would book anything again.

Time and time again I've been told that this is a business, and it's all about relationships. I agree, but like many things it's easier said than done. For years I maintained files of casting directors, ad agencies, producers, production houses, and corporate in-house production facilities. I sent a demo tape to anyone who might possibly pay me to talk. I had some success, but not much. It's part of the process. If you don't have an agent, you've got to do these things. Now I work out of an ISDN studio in my home. I collaborate with my agents to provide opportunities and I do my best to book what I can. I have to say, some people market themselves very assertively, and certainly for a few it has paid off.

Years ago, I was experiencing a self-imposed lull between agents. I wasn't getting much work, and the debt was piling up. There were children to feed and bills to pay. I had finally lined up a meeting with an agent whom I believed could help me unlock the door to success. I was wearing an old charcoal gray Hugo Boss suit. It had a couple of holes in the sleeve from a moth that had moved into the storage bag, but before I went to the meeting my wife colored the holes with a black magic marker. Soon after the meeting began, the agent lifted his hands, made a box frame with his fingers, and framed my face from across the desk.

"You're so stiff," he said. "You just don't sound like you enjoy life. Have you considered another line of work?"

I felt a pit in my stomach and a rush of blood to my head. I stood up, informed him that I would be successful in this business with or without him, and left the building feeling completely dejected. The experience made me question what I was putting my family through. I truly didn't know if I would make it, but I wanted it so badly. I love this business. I always have.

How did I overcome the experience?

I just never gave up.

Over time you learn that just because you don't book a job, it doesn't mean that anyone has a problem with you as a person. When it comes to emotions, it's important to separate your voice as a product from yourself as a person. That being said, there are several things that can affect me—and that have. Years ago when finances were a constant concern, the need to book more work did affect my auditions. I put so much pressure on myself that my reads were tight. It was difficult to relax and just throw it out there, come what may. I don't recall ever feeling like people were saying, oh no, not him again. But I do remember feeling more fragile emotionally.

Let's face it—most people don't book a majority of their auditions. So as long as I can pay the bills, I try not to worry about it. Except for the big ones—I still hate losing out on the big ones. One that I will always remember was the time an ad agency flew me out to Los Angeles to audition for a national account. It was the second audition, and they had narrowed the field to five of us. A week or so later they brought me back again with the field pared to three. This would have been a huge account, but in the end I didn't get the job. My therapist says I'm doing much better now—just kidding. I've booked some pretty good jobs over the years and have no complaints. I've been blessed.

I've worked with several voice coaches. One in particular was a casting director who had me read scripts using numerous emotions. In one read, I was speaking to an audience of several hundred people. A different one had me talking to a group of kindergarten children. And another had me gently talking to a widow at her husband's funeral. Yet the script never changed. She helped me to choose a point of origin. Once I've identified the emotion, I try to go there in my head. It helps to make the read real. Don't think about how your voice sounds. If you have the emotion, the voice will follow.

People will hear what you feel. If you smile, they can hear it. If you are relaxed, they will hear that, too. I can honestly say that I've probably blown a lot of auditions over the years because I needed the work. I was thinking too much about the need for money and not enough about staying relaxed and giving my best read. Just do your best to make it real. Then whatever happens happens. One time I was up against some well-known voice-over guys for a commercial. The audition was at an ad agency in New York. When my turn came around, they led me into a boardroom with this huge table. The clients and the ad people were at one end of the table. At the other end was a lone microphone stand with no place to lay down the script. I said hello, gave my name, and started to read. Within seconds I realized my hand was shaking too badly to read the copy. So I stopped and asked if I could tape the script to the back of a chair so it would stay still long enough for me to read it. They agreed; I took a deep breath, closed my eyes, and gave a long relaxing exhale. Then I just let it go. A couple of weeks later my agent called; I had booked the job.

It's always a combination of things a voice-over artist must do to find work. You accumulate more and more contacts as time goes by. Some are the result of professional relationships and some are personal. Sometimes you book a job from a casting director who didn't think you were right for one job, but who remembered you and thought you would be perfect for another. A relationship with an agency is a partnership. They do well when you do well. It's important to demonstrate that you're committed and that you don't just sit around and wait for things to be handed to you. If you want to have access to the good auditions, you will need to have a good relationship with an agent. Think of the agent as your business partner. And remember, that job isn't easy either.

Voice-over artistry is a part of who I am. If I'm watching television, I'll automatically pay attention to both the promo and commercial spots. I'll think about how I might have done it differently or maybe I'll learn something by realizing how well it was done. It's always strange when you hear a spot on the air that you read for, and the read is completely different from the direction you were given at the audition.

I've had a studio in my home for almost seven years now; you can't beat the commute. And being the voice of *Law & Order* has allowed me to make some civic contributions, like serving as a co-host of the Top Cops Awards, which I've been doing for about five years. It's amazing to meet and talk with the real heroes. I can also lend my voice to worthwhile organizations like Tuesday's Children, a group dedicated to helping the children of 9/11 victims.

Having a great voice is nice, but it's only the beginning. It's like saying, hey, I have a really nice piano so I should be able to play it, right? Well maybe you can and maybe you can't. If you have a great voice, it may sound nice, but can you play it? Can you take a script and make it come alive the way a musician might read music and bring it to life? Some people are naturally gifted and can play by ear, but if you're not one of them, you'll have to learn how to play your gift the old fashion way—by training. When you're watching television or listening to the radio, pay attention to the styles that are booking the jobs and listen for changes in trends. I really think you have to love this business to make it a career. You have to make a lot of sacrifices along the way. It gets tough when most of your buddies have good jobs and you're still banging your head against the wall.

Unexpectedly, several years ago Dick Wolf called and asked me to read an opening narration for a new show called *Law & Order*. I had played a small role as a detective in the pilot episode and had done some other work with him prior to that. During that time we had become friends. Dick stood next to me during the session and told me exactly how he wanted the opening to sound. I had no idea those few words would lead to where I am today. Sometimes it just takes a little luck or being in the right place at the right time.

When this voice has announced its last promo or commercial or whatever, I'd like to be remembered as a nice guy, a loving husband, and a good father. Anything else is just a bonus. On the other hand, I've often wondered what I would be doing had things not worked out in the voice-over business. I don't know the answer, but it's a depressing thought. If the day ever comes that I can no longer communicate, well, I guess I just wouldn't be me anymore.

2nd SECRET

To gain access to auditions for the top brands, you will need to have a good relationship with an agent. Think of your agent as your business partner and remember, that job isn't easy either.

Hattie Winston

Hattie Winston is a TV star on *Becker*. Her voice-over credits include: *Rugrats: All Growed Up*, American Airlines, Revlon, Burger King, Jamaican Tourism, and Bahamas Tourism.

ALTHOUGH I HAVE BEEN A SUCCESSFUL VOICE-OVER ACTOR FOR WELL OVER twenty years, I find that the struggle continues. I can only speculate as to the reasons why, although in some instances they have been made quite plain. Because I am African American, it is often assumed that I can only voice so-called "ethnic" characters. My background is theatre, particularly the New York stage. When I was young, I was fortunate to be mentored by one of the best voice-over actors ever—Adolph Caesar. It was he who encouraged me to study and develop my vocal technique. It was, in fact, Adolph who introduced me to his agent, Angela DiPene at Cunningham,

Escott, Slevin & DiPene in New York. I had had representation in other areas and occasionally would be sent out on voice-over auditions, but I did not have an agency whose very area of expertise was commercials.

It took patience, courage, confidence, and a lot of leg work for me to develop into a working voice talent. It took patience because there were many times I went on auditions (as we used to do in New York City where it's not just an agent submitting a tape of a client) when I would not be seen by the clients, or assumptions were made about my abilities before I was even heard. Fortunately, I had developed a reputation as an on-camera artist, so in some instances the transition was made easier.

Of course, with my first demo tape I had no clue since I had never done voice-overs. I had no product, so I had to listen to tapes of clients at my new agency and then choose material from existing television and radio spots and try to do my interpretation of the copy. I needed lots of help putting the tape together.

As stated above, a very good friend of mine, Adolph Caesar, who was one of the top voice-over artists—if not the top—in New York City at that time, introduced me to his representatives. They knew of my work on Broadway and other theaters as well as my on-camera work, and they agreed to sign me.

When selling myself, my first attempt is to have the casting people throw away their preconceived notions of what I can or cannot do. I am the product that I am selling; I am the owner of my business of which I am the CEO. So, therefore, my approach is: "Let's get the product out there." Sometimes that involves mailings; sometimes it simply means reminding my agency that I exist.

When I first began working in New York City, I was sent to audition for the voice of a well-known beauty product. They were looking for a spokesperson, i.e., the person who would be contracted to promote that particular product. I had a relationship with the ad agency that was handling the product, so they requested me. I went in and thought I did well, but I was told that they could not use me—not because of my work but because of my color. (You must remember this was before James Earl Jones or Ruby Dee or Halle Berry). I was devastated. But I decided, after I recovered from the humiliation, that I would never again use my photo on my reel. Instead, I designed a lovely pink lion logo and used that instead. I decided that I would be ferocious (like a lion) in my pursuit for other voice-over work.

To be rejected is to be cast away, discarded, and deemed unacceptable. When this happens, it has a tremendous impact. With each rejection, hopefully a new resolve is formulated, but this has not always been the case with me. Sometimes, I feel that my voice-over rejections are more emotionally negative because I see my voice as coming from the very essence of who I am. It is not just this instrument I use to make something out of nothing but rather the essence of who I am. My soul, if you will, is on display. And if this is rejected, then surely the rest of the package is unacceptable as well. People may not realize it, but when it is just you and a microphone in a booth, you are naked, exposed . . . there are no external props to assist you. My voice (my soul) is reverberating in the earphones, coming back at me, saying, "Yes, you are doing a good job." And when that is rejected, can you believe in yourself anymore? Of course you can, I'm still here and still working!

I'm not certain I have a specific technique, except to be specific about who this character is, what I'm selling, and what the copy is ultimately attempting to say. I must also understand the audience to whom I am speaking.

As stated earlier, race has been an obstacle and continues to be one. When I am selling to an African American demographic, I'm told I'm not black enough—and when I'm selling to a generic, i.e., white, American market . . . I'm sometimes told my ethnicity is too obvious! Now the choice is just to be who I am, with the knowledge I have gained over these years.

My work comes primarily from my agents here in L.A. The approach here is completely different from New York City. There I believe you can build relationships with ad agencies, casting directors, engineers, product managers, and others who have seen you over the years, know what you're capable of, and therefore can see or recommend you for different jobs. Here in L.A. though, it's up to the agency, and if they see you one way, then that's the way you're auditioned.

Once when I was working on the show *Becker* and I was introduced to a young actor, he began to tell me how I had had a great influence on his life and work via a voice-over job I'd done many years before. I was fortunate to have done the entire narrative for a PBS documentary on Louis

Armstrong. Mr. Armstrong was his favorite artist, and he had watched that show over and over through the years and found encouragement because of it. As a matter of fact, he later took on a project about Mr. Armstrong and told me that he listened to my voice almost on a weekly basis. That made me feel good!

Study, study, study! One of my favorite activities is trying to recognize the names of the voice-over actors who are on TV. It's very interesting to me to hear the voices of some of our movie stars who are now doing voice-over work. I remember when doing commercial work, whether on-camera or off, was looked on with disdain. Now everyone is doing it. And the question remains—what about the artists who have been doing this work who are now unemployed because big name stars are now being paid incredible sums of money? Does the general public really know the difference?

The most unexpected thing that has come out of being a voice-over artist is that I am still doing this. When Adolph Caesar told me all those years ago that I could make a living at it, I'm not so certain I believed him. I have learned so much about myself in all those booths I've been in! I've also served as national co-chair of AFTRA's Equal Employment Opportunities Committee.

I want my voice to be remembered as the voice that you could trust whenever you listened to it, no matter the product. To not be able to communicate coherently is unimaginable.

3rd SECRET

Find a mentor who is knowledgeable about the voice-over industry. Trust this person to be an objective observer of the choices you make in pursuit of your career.

Joe Cipriano

Joe Cipriano is a broadcast veteran. He has been the promo voice of the Fox Television comedies for seventeen years and the CBS comedies for the past eight years. He has worked on the air for NBC, ABC, and CBS. His live announcer credits include the Grammy Awards, the Blockbuster Entertainment Awards, VH1 Honors, *GQ* magazine's Men of the Year Awards, and many more.

THE FIRST TIME I MADE A VOICE-OVER DEMO TAPE, I WAS WORKING AS A RADIO personality at ABC in Washington, D.C. As part of my on-air shift, I had to make copies of the commercials that came into the station from ad agencies and recording studios for broadcast. It occurred to me that wherever these tapes came from might be a good place to start trying to find voice-over work of my own. So I wrote down the name and address of every ad agency and recording studio the tapes came from and sent my demo to them. My first demos essentially were made up of fake commercials I thought might help me get work. Because I worked in radio, I had access to a recording studio at the station late at night to record my fake voice-over demo. It was this process, which I repeated over and over again throughout my early years of pursuing voice-over, that got me my first jobs in the business. Of course, once I starting working periodically as a voice talent, I was then able to take those real commercials I'd done and add them to my demo reel. I remember with pride the first time I actually had a demo reel that was made up of genuine commercials I'd been paid to do. It took a while, but it was a great feeling of accomplishment.

I started my voice-over career in Washington, D.C., which is a major broadcasting and regional commercial production market, but, surprisingly, at that time there were no voice-over agents per se. In fact, everyone in the business in that area pretty much sought out work on their own through mailings, phone calls, and a grass roots type of marketing directly to ad agencies and recording studios. I was somewhat successful, but it didn't take long to realize that the big gigs weren't being cast in Washington. Sure, there was a lot of local and regional commercial work there, and many area performers have very successful careers, but it was my dream to get into network television and be heard from coast to coast. I wanted to represent something considered All American. It inspired and drove me. But I knew I had to be in New York City or Los Angeles to achieve my goal, or at least to have a shot at it.

Adhering to my golden rule of voice-overs, "Never make a move without having a job waiting for you," I started looking for radio jobs in Los Angeles and finally got an afternoon job there at KHTZ. When my wife Ann and I arrived, she got a job right away at KABC TV as a news writer and segment producer. I began searching for an agent and constructed demo tapes from some of the commercials I'd done in Washington—only this time putting my voice into fake national commercials in the KHTZ studios to make me sound more big time. I employed my same routine, writing down the addresses of ad agencies and recording studios from the tapes that came into the radio station and sending out my new demo. Of course, in L.A. you *have* to have an agent if you're serious about pursuing a voice-over career. So my demo tapes went out not only to ad agencies but also to every voice-over agent on the AFTRA agents' list as well.

I found my first agent at Commercials Unlimited, where I got some auditions and made some gains, but I continued to look for more prominent representation. Then I found Vanessa Gilbert at Talent Group Inc. She was the perfect first agent because she was new to the business herself and had great ideas for marketing her clients, including setting up voice-over workshops with guest directors from casting agencies. Thanks to Vanessa, I attended my first workshops and actually started scoring a few gigs. Vanessa has since become a very prominent agent with the Tisherman Agency in Los Angeles where she handles millions of dollars of work each year.

Although Talent Group was a good start, it wasn't until I moved to Nina Nisenholtz at the William Morris Agency that I started booking bigger gigs. I did the trailers and commercials for the movie *Fast Times at Ridgemont High*, which became a cult classic, as well as the trailers for a few other early '80s movies such as *Porkys* and *Porkys II*, and an early Tom Cruise movie, *All the Right Moves*. I even did a national on-camera TV commercial for Prego Spaghetti Sauce. Prego flew me to New York to shoot the spot in a suburban New Jersey home with Estelle Harris (George Castanza's mother on *Seinfeld*). We stirred spaghetti sauce at the kitchen stove while she asked me whether there were fresh tomatoes and basil and oregano in my sauce, and I responded to each query with the Prego tag line, "It's in there." It was a cute spot. That's when it first dawned on me that even though I might "sound" All American, I "looked" like an Italian kid, which wouldn't translate to many All American on-camera opportunities for me.

Once I moved from William Morris to the Tisherman Agency, I really started making a living in voice-overs. It was there I learned that a good agency can benefit you through the trickle down theory. As one of the top voice-over agents, they get a lot of calls for auditions. So sometimes I'd get gigs simply because the buyer's first choice wasn't available, and they trickled down to me. Another advantage of being with a top agency is the fact that their house reel gets listened to a lot, and you can score gigs off the reel. After seven years with Tisherman, I had a second meeting with Rita Vennari at Sutton, Barth and Vennari, where I reminded her that she had turned me down for representation seven years ago. This time I was a seven-figure talent, and I guess I came in with a little more heat. I'd always liked Rita a lot, as well as her staff, and the timing seemed right. So I moved to SBV and began working with the great agents there, including my number one confidant, Mary Ellen Lord, whom I talk to countless times each day.

By the way, if you ever decide to change agents, please have the guts to have a face-to-face talk with your agent. Don't be a weenie and call on the phone and say, "I'm leaving." That's just not right. I respect the work agents do for clients; I don't like jumping from agency to agency, and for the past eighteen years, I've only had two agents, Steve Tisherman and Rita Vennari.

Self-promotion is essential in order to make yourself heard above the deafening sound of voice-over talent screaming for attention. At the beginning of my career, I tried everything I could think of to make my demo and name stand out. One time, I sent out a series of postcards to every agent and casting person for whom I had an address in Washington, D.C. and L.A. For two weeks, the series, which was printed on oversized cards that stood out in the recipient's mailbox, told a story or built suspense. The serial began with the first card on Monday saying, "There's a new voice in town . . ." By Friday, another card arrived that said, " . . . a voice that is youthful, warm, friendly and energetic . . ." This went on for another week with short descriptions of this "new voice." Within a week or so, the last card would arrive in an envelope along with my voice-over demo and the revelation that this new voice was a guy named Joe Cipriano. Pretty lame in retrospect, but it worked to an extent. It did make me stand out, and I did get some work from it and was called in by several agents. One agent told me that she knew a Joe Cipriano when she was growing up who happened to be a famous baseball player. Two days later I had a box delivered to her office. In it was a baseball autographed by me. I signed it "The other Joe Cipriano." She became my first on-camera agent. I also used to send scratch pads to everyone with my name and my agent's name and phone number on them. The point being that I hoped my name would seep into their brains by osmosis. Printed on each page of the pad was: "Joe Cipriano, The Voice that Speaks for Itself." Whatever the hell that meant.

The voice-over business was not at all as I expected it to be. A voice-over career is like a roller coaster—a long slow climb up to that first crest and then the inevitable drop. The ups get higher and the drops get shallower once you hit a certain stride, but it's never a smooth ride. The first experience that brought me to my knees, so to speak, was towards the beginning of my stint with the FOX Network. I'd been hired in 1988 by the head of on-air promos, Bob Bibb, who had heard me on the air at KIIS FM. He called the radio station from his car to find out who my agent was.

Funny, after all those years of sending demos, postcards, and pads, I finally got a break thanks to good old radio. I started with FOX in the summer of 1988, just one year after they had hit the air. It was a struggling network for sure, and most people told me not to get too excited about the gig because the network would fold by the end of the year. A show called *Married with Children* changed that, followed soon after by a little cartoon called *The Simpsons,* and the NFL on FOX.

My long ride to the first peak of the roller coaster was an eight-year chug from the moment Ann and I arrived in Los Angeles in December 1980. I finally reached the coaster's first plateau by becoming the voice of all the comedy promos for FOX. The job brought me more money than I could ever imagine and in the process changed the sound of network promo. The network promo status quo up till then had been the big deep-voiced type of announcer like Ernie Anderson. My arrival initiated a change in Imaging for Networks who, once they saw FOX's success, changed their own imaging by adding bolder, hotter graphics and hiring voice talent with a lighter, younger, more real sound. So, as I was enjoying the air on the roller coaster summit for a few years, FOX hired a new head of creative, complete with ponytail, whose name I have completely blocked from memory. He assigned a new look and feel to the network, with a different voice for every show. I went from being the promo voice of something like ten shows a week to one: *Married with Children.* My income dropped 90 percent in one fell swoop, and I got a good taste of how fickle this whole business is and how little control you actually have over your fate. It's scary, to say the least. Fortunately, it didn't last long, Mr. Ponytail was let go in short order, and I was lucky enough to get those shows back thanks to people like Sandy Grushow, Geoff Calnan, and Ron Scalera, who thought I had something to offer. That first drop in the roller coaster is always the one you remember: There's nothing but free fall and fright. Thank God, after hitting the bottom of that first drop, the trip back up the next hill began.

It's true that relationships in this business go a long way. When Ron Scalera left FOX in 1997 to become head of marketing at CBS, he took me along, and I was lucky enough to become the new comedy voice of CBS. I've been with CBS during what I call their "worst to first" campaign. In 1997, CBS was considered a senior citizen's TV network. In the 2004

November sweeps, it not only celebrated a one-year anniversary as the most watched TV network in America, it also won the coveted eighteen to forty-nine year-old demographic. It's a success story of programming and marketing coming together at a very high level.

My experience going from ten shows to one at FOX is a scare that can haunt a person day and night for the rest of one's career. It's inevitable that it's all going to end, but when? How long can this go on? It's humbling, frightening, and exciting all at the same time. I've heard artists, singers, and actors from all fields express the same opinion about their own careers: "Someday they're going to find me out, and someone is going to grab me by the shoulder and shout, 'Hey, how did *you* get in here?'" It's tied to another experience that weaves its way through this whole profession—that little bit of joy called rejection. You audition and are rejected countless times throughout your career. The only way to handle it is to convince yourself that it's not personal. You are not being rejected; your performance, your sound or your type is being rejected. It's tough to separate yourself from your type or your sound though because it's such a part of who you are. I've never had big problems with rejection because these decisions are made from personal taste in the casting process. They're looking for a particular sound or look, and if you don't have it, you're not asked to be a part of the project. It hurts more because you're missing out on a job rather than because of the rejection itself, don't you think?

I put my emphasis on properly and inventively interpreting the copy, which always has been more or less on a gut level. I've done thousands of network TV promos, and I'm at my best when I can bring my energy, genuine excitement, and personality to the project. Obviously what I do in my performance is driven by the thirty-second story being told to entice viewers to watch this particular show on Sunday night at eight. I'm fortunate because I'm genuinely excited about my work, partially because I'm living that dream of talking to America and also because it's fun. Promo writers and producers begin developing a concept to sell a show by viewing the episode and choosing the story line to highlight and the best jokes without giving away too much. By the time these promos are ready to read, they've been scrutinized by some of the best people in network marketing. The source material in the promo comes from the pen of some of the top comedy writers in the business, and it's presented in promo form by the best minds in marketing. So I'm reading to a promo that's pretty damn enter-taining. What I bring to it is energy, excitement, and honesty. The viewer should be struck by how funny the show is going to be Sunday night and how incredibly excited this guy is to tell you about it. Job done.

Network marketing is a cutting edge business, yet it is still evolving. I've been fortunate not to have to deal with negative racial attitudes or big-otry, although, surprisingly, stereotypical attitudes have held back women in voice-over for years. Somewhere along the line, some people got it in their heads that announcers are men, not women. But thankfully I've seen women battle this antiquated attitude and win. There was even a time in radio when there were no female disc jockeys. In fact, there was a standing order, a programming edict that you *never* played two female artists back to back on radio. I'm not kidding, this was a programming no-no. I'm heart-ened by the fact that women have fought off this attitude in the TV and radio broadcasting field and I hope that soon women in voice-overs, pro-mos especially, will be treated equally. It's silly to think a man's voice can be used to sell a product or show geared towards men and also sell those geared towards women. At the same time, it's thought that a female voice artist can only voice promos for female-only programming. I don't agree with such old stereotypical thinking and am very happy to see it fade. It's changing—very slowly, but it is changing.

Finding work in this business is a never-ending quest. Thankfully, as my friend and voice-over actor George DelHoyo says, "Work begets work." The more you do, the more people you meet, the more casting people hear the work you've done, the more you are cast. Not to say it's all that easy. There is another strange problem that occurs and that is when you're on the air so much casting people start to think you're overused. You've heard the joke about the five stages of a voice-over career, haven't you? It goes like this:

Stage 1: Who is Joe Cipriano?
Stage 2: Get me Joe Cipriano.
Stage 3: Get me Joe Cipriano at any price.
Stage 4: Get me a young Joe Cipriano.
Stage 5: Who is Joe Cipriano?

Depending on my voice to make a living is very interesting. "Graduate of Harvard" on my résumé wouldn't mean much in my business. I feel kinship to Bing Crosby, who made a living with his voice yet always made it look easy. Truth is, it all seemed so easy because it *was* easy—for him. Other people who don't have that wonderful gift have to work much harder to fulfill their aspirations. My voice would have been a hindrance to me twenty-five years ago when *big* was in. The timing of my arrival was fortunate, since my voice is just right for what I'm paid to do—exciting, high energy, youthful, fun voice-over work. How fortunate. How lucky I am.

Because of this easygoing attitude I have toward work and my career, I lead an easygoing life as well. I have a wonderful wife, Ann, and two great kids, Dayna and Alex, and we live a harmonious life. What you see is what you get. We all know successful people who've had to do some pretty horrible things in their careers to make it to where they are, often at the cost of a marriage and a relationship with their children. When I think about how my voice-over career has affected other aspects of my life, I can say that it's made me thankful for what I have. It's also made me realize how fragile it all is, as well as how important it is to appreciate every aspect of life as it's happening.

People often ask me for advice for upcoming voice-over artists or artists who aren't working enough to make ends meet. First of all, if you quit your job when you decide to become a voice-over artist, you're in big trouble. Throughout all levels in my career I've always had another job outside of voice-overs. When you're starting out, you must have a day job, any job, that pays the rent, and then after that job is done each day, you have several hours left over to devote one hundred percent of that time to becoming a voice-over artist. In my case, my day job was radio. I always kept a radio job until the day came when it was evident that voice-over jobs were contributing to the lion's share of my income. And only then, with great trepidation, did I quit my day job and rely on voice-overs a hundred percent.

Mark Elliot, a former radio guy and the comedy voice at CBS for many years, scared the hell out of me a long time ago. I used to sit in on audio room sessions where the network promos were voiced, mixed, and readied for air, watching Mark, Chuck Riley, and others do a slew of network promos in one sitting. I learned how writers and producers prepared their

JOE CIPRIANO

promos and how post-production producers directed the talent and over-saw the day-to-day work in the studio. During one visit, Mark told me two things: Never take a vacation or you'll lose your gig to the guy who fills in for you and never buy a house based on voice-over income.

Wow. That got me thinking, "Why the hell do I wanna do this gig?" I learned that Mark was correct, but you've got to take chances, too. Bob Bibb hired me to fill in at FOX because the previous artist took a two-week vacation, and I got what's been a sixteen-year gig—not solely because of the vacation, but it certainly contributed to my first big break. Maybe that's why I was one of the first voice-over artists to utilize ISDN. With an ISDN telephone connection and equipment, an announcer can work essentially anywhere in the world. Since the technology became available in 1994, I not only installed an ISDN studio in my house, I also encouraged FOX to purchase ISDN equipment as well so I could leave town without losing the gig. We take vacations, but I do at least a one-hour session each workday via an ISDN line. I've worked from hotel rooms in Hawaii, Colorado, Arizona, Connecticut, Italy, a studio in London England, an NPR radio station in Washington D.C., and just about everywhere I've gone with my family in the past twelve years. I've found that I can take a holiday—as long as I work a little.

So go after your dreams, but keep your day job. Let it finance your quest because any actor who goes into an audition or meeting frantically needing that job has the stench of desperation on him—an aroma casting directors, agents and, producers are very sensitive to. Go in feeling confident, eager, and in control, and you will further your career much faster.

My first acting teacher in Los Angeles, Wayne Dvorak, told a story one day that always stayed with me. He asked, "Why do some people make it, while others don't?" There are many answers, but his story was this: When you work towards your dream, a little red light glows on top of your head. When you stop or are distracted, the light dims or goes off completely. It's important to keep the light glowing brightly and consistently. Why? Because the Gods of Making Dreams Come True are sitting up there in the heavens looking down. Their joy is to help people fulfill their dreams. They just need to know how much you want it, and they can only see you if your red light is *on*. So, keep working at your dream. Devote one hour a day, that's all—just one hour a day—but make it *every* day, and do something that moves you towards your goal. Whether it's a workshop, or study, or writing cards and letters, or working on your demo or making calls, whatever it is, do it for one hour every day. You'll be amazed at how you'll make progress, and your light will shine brightly. You'll make it easy for the Gods of Making Dreams Come True to find you.

The most unexpected thing to come out of being a voice-over artist is that sometimes people actually know my name or recognize my voice. Voice-overs are a pretty anonymous endeavor—just a voice in the dark, so to speak. It's a wonderful career that way. If you're a success, the financial and creative benefits are numerous, yet the *National Enquirer* will never write a nasty tell-all article about you, and you're never stalked by paparazzi. The latter may be due to what I call the "face for radio" syndrome. I'm not entirely serious when I say that, but I do think that most voice-over actors are better heard and not seen.

I hope that my voice is remembered as warm, enthusiastic, fun, and honest, which is also the way I hope I'm remembered. "Call Me Lucky" might be written on my grave. I found the love of my life at an early age and helped raise two of the most wonderful people I've ever met. I treasure my family and my friends.

Someone asked me once what I thought it would be like if I were to lose my voice, to become speechless. It's a scary thought. I think it would be like a prison, but the human spirit is formidable, and within time I would find a way to communicate somehow. My Dad passed away at eighty-eight from complications due to dementia. At the end of his life, he wasn't able to communicate except with some facial expression, his eyes, and sometimes with a laugh. Now that he's gone, I still hear him coming out of me. Sometimes I'll cough, clear my throat, or laugh, and it's the exact sound he used to make. Certain words I say remind me of his intonation. So I guess in the end he really wasn't silenced. His voice still lives on in me somehow.

4th SECRET

It's rare that a beginning voice-over actor can pay the rent by voice-over work alone. Be prepared to support yourself financially while putting in the time to develop your craft.

Joan Baker

Joan Baker narrated, in tandem with President Bill Clinton, a documentary about the founding of the William Jefferson Clinton Library, now a part of the library's permanent display, and voiced a PSA campaign series introducing the Muhammad Ali Center. Other clients include: American Express, HBO Family, ABC News, ESPN Classic, Bloomberg TV & Radio, Sony Music, JPMorgan Chase, and Simon & Schuster Audio.

IT ALL STARTED WITH SIX SUITCASES AND A DANCE BAG THAT ACCOMPANIED me from California to New York City when I was nineteen years old. After two excruciating years of training in Alvin Ailey's scholarship program, I noticed that I had never managed—and no one else had either for that matter—to move from my scholarship designation to joining the first company. So I asked the school to assess my talent and potential, so that I could figure this thing out. After all, I had been training as a dancer my whole life and I was here to dance, for God's sake! The unexpected reply I got couldn't have been more perplexing and shocking and, truth be told, it plagued me for years to follow: "Your biracial look is not marketable enough." *Could it be that I'm not black enough or not white enough to pursue my lifelong dream of being an accomplished dancer?* Though I was in a state of shock and disbelief, I decided I'd better diversify my talent base. I continued my dance training through independent schools but folded in acting lessons to pursue my second childhood dream of performing on the big screen.

However, when I began my search for an agent, I was smacked with the same basic analysis. One prominent talent agent (whom I'd love to name but probably shouldn't) looked me up and down—scanning my complexion and facial features with a decidedly puzzled expression—and uttered, "What exactly are you?" Innocent and naïve as I was, I hadn't fully understood or connected the marketability problem in the dance world with the acting world.

"I'm mixed . . . I'm biracial," I said.

"You're a beautiful girl, very exotic and all, but your look isn't marketable."

Didn't anyone realize this was my life's dream they were chalking up to a lack of marketability? Didn't anyone realize that marketability was the label they were putting on my one basket of eggs? I was devastated, mortified, and up stage creek without a curtain call. But more than anything, I was in need of a career.

I didn't pick voice-over; I think voice-over picked me. I was at a very low point in my dance and acting career. I was broke with no income in sight and waiting for an answer to fall out of the sky. Interestingly enough, the last job I'd had was as an entertainment correspondent for a short-lived cable show where they had me deliver my reports in a sort of ditzy character voice. Already the whole voice thing was starting to call me.

Flipping later through *Backstage*, it called again. I saw an ad for learning to do voice-over with Joni Robbins. She offered training in character voices and using one's real voice. Well, the character voices were already something in line with stuff that came easy to me, and I figured I couldn't go wrong with a woman who had my name so I gave it a spin. Little did I know that this invisible trade would became my ticket out of racial type casting (sort of) and finally into a professional career in the entertainment industry. And, surprisingly enough, my dance and acting training proved to be critical to my initial entrée into this very complex craft. But I was a long, long way from success, and getting there took unstoppable determination.

I was enamored by the one-on-one coaching and by Joni's pearls of wisdom. And I loved the fact that she seemed to take a genuine interest in me. I felt like it was my responsibility to take what she was teaching me and to do something great with it. She taught me about the relationship between my vocal expression and the microphone from a performance perspective and trained me to interpret various kinds of scripts. There was a great deal more to learn after this initial training, but I began to learn how to channel my vocal talents into the voice-over craft.

The next step was to create a voice-over demo tape—an absolute necessity in the business—and I learned a valuable lesson right off: namely, that I would have to create good work even though I had a horrible cold on the day I recorded it. I was literally leaving the room after each take to cough and clear my nose. But the director, Joni, and Cinema Sound's engineer, Jon, fully guided me, and you would never know from listening to this tape that I was as sick as a dog. As a performer, trust your instincts and your instrument, but trust the direction and coaching of your professionals. They made all the difference in achieving a high quality result.

Now I had to package the tape—to come up with a thematic graphic look that would represent my personality and help my tape stand out. So my very artistic roommate created a caricature of me as a logo—a sort of a barfly girl sitting on a stool smoking a cigarette. It was very funny, and we used it for the tape, the tape case, and the cover letter. It's been revised a bit, but it still serves as my logo after all these years. Since I hadn't yet recognized voice-over as a career, I planned to use the tape as a piece in my arsenal of pursuing acting work—a "Hey, look what else I can do" proposition. I had no idea of the highly competitive, dog-eat-dog world of professional voice-over. As it turns out, naiveté is sometimes your best friend.

After years beating the pavement as an actor, I knew where to find the talent agents who might audition my new demo. I'd start with the top agencies and work my way down. Also—I dropped everything off in person. This way you actually get to meet people (even receptionists can make the difference) and be assured that the package arrives, which makes following up easier. The personal attention also makes it more likely that someone hears your CD. Agents are extremely busy, inundated with more calls and contacts than they can answer in one day. So, when you mail everything in, you're lucky if it even gets opened within two or three weeks or months, and by that time it's at the bottom of the pile.

I dropped off my tape with Don Buchwald and Associates, J Michael Bloom, Cunningham, Escott, Slevin & Dipene, Abrams Artists, and a couple of others. On the elevator to Abrams Artists, a very dapper man asked me if I was going to Abrams. I told him yes, that I was dropping off my voice-over demo. He gave me an expression as if to say my chances were one in a billion, but I wasn't discouraged. The guy, however, bolted off the elevator ahead of me as soon as we got to Abrams' floor. I dropped off my tape with the receptionist, was as friendly as I could be, and headed back to the elevator. Before I reached it, an agent (Dave Evans) came out his door, ran after me, and asked if I was Joan Baker. He said he would like to meet with me and invited me into his office where he put on my tape. Within ten seconds, he stopped it and said, "This is great." Then he grabbed his phone and said to his secretary, "Hold all my calls!"

"I can't believe this is all you," he said, referring to my tape, "Can I send you out on an audition tomorrow?"

"Of course," I said. It was a dream come true! Then he asked me if I was related to the man who had rushed into his office before me, and I told him that I'd just now met the guy on the elevator. The agent then told me that the "elevator guy" was so determined that I get in to see him that Dave had thought I was a blood relative, and that that was the reason he'd come out to see me! As it turned out, the elevator guy was a six-figure voice-over talent and a top client.

Later that day I learned that three other agencies wanted to sign me based on my demo, and I made appointments to meet with them all. In the meantime, I went on a few auditions with Abrams until I finally decided on Don Buchwald and Associates because they were the most aggressive in reaching out to me, and because of an amazing conversation I had with one of their agents, Robyn Stecher, who became my signing agent. She said she felt I would truly be successful as a voice-over artist, and though all the other agents had to agree, she was going to push for me to be signed. This was music to my ears. You have to remember I was a complete novice still thinking this is a great step in the direction of acting. And the one thing that had been plaguing me as an actress—being biracial—never came up.

Advertisers target very specific demographics when they create ads. When someone of mixed race cannot be easily categorized as one race or another, it misses the advertiser's objective. As a result, I was often turned away because it was felt that viewers would be confused by not being able to discern my race. And it was deeply distressing for me since all I ever wanted was to have a career in show business. So I was grateful that it hadn't come up when signing with Buchwald, and I certainly wasn't going to bring it up. Later I realized race was less an issue because voice-over artists are heard, not seen. I emphasize *less* because race is something that can be distinguished through vocal quality, enunciation, and so forth. Fortunately, I had no regionalisms or ill-defined voice qualities that would have created a distinct audio category like black, urban, or Southern, which made me a more versatile commodity. I must admit, though, that in my heart I still want a career that allows me to be seen.

At present a big piece of my career is in the hands of an outstanding agent by the name of Shari Hoffman at Innovative Artists. Shari has been the consummate advocate and an ally as well. I think our agent/client relationship works as well as it does because we both bring a great deal of experience to the table. My path to finding my first agent was very unique because not many people drop off a reel and get signed one week later. On the other hand, there are certain things one can do to bolster the chances of securing an agent in voice-over:

- Study with a reputable voice-over artist who teaches private classes.
- Take classes in improvisation, on-camera commercials, and scene study at private acting schools.
- Create and package your reel demo so that it cuts through the competition and expresses your uniqueness.
- Learn which agents handle voice-over and get your package (and yourself) in front of them.

Once you have an agent, the relationship will develop based upon your and the agent's personalities. Count on your agent to manage you in a professional way. Take his or her advice to heart and assume that the relationship is going the way it should, especially if you're new to the business.

It may not be anything like you thought it would be, so you'll just have to trust that it is what it's supposed to be. Over time you will learn how to develop the relationship to new levels. But be as self-sufficient as possible generating your voice-over career. Your agent has many talented voice artists to manage and business to negotiate and can't possibly address your daily concerns and insecurities, take all your calls, or give you feedback after every audition.

Learn how to market yourself, network, and enter the business circle. When you go on an audition, it's up to you to spot and create conversational openings that could lead you to handing your package directly to a casting agent, director, or producer. Networking is not always about making the sale. Sometimes it's just about enjoying other people and sharing yourself—typical dinnertime conversation. It's work you as a voice-over artist do, not work your agent can do. However, you do want to keep your agent abreast of your significant contacts for appropriate follow up. This way both of you can work together connecting the dots to the opportunities.

Clearly, not all agents bring the same expertise and talent to the job. As a novice, don't focus on judging your agent as much as on creating a genuine working relationship. In time, and from discussing agent/client relationships with other levelheaded clients and agents, you will learn everything you need to know about creating a working relationship.

When Robyn Stecher first signed me to Buchwald, one of the first things I asked was how to get myself before the people doing all the hiring. She gave me her entire Rolodex (Shhhh! Don't tell anybody), and I introduced myself to each and every creative director and producer in it. I went to their offices, waited in lobbies, met receptionists, and made friends with security guards and doormen. Sometimes my new friends would point out a passing producer, and I'd introduce myself and give my VO package. Sometimes, I even got auditions and bookings!

When it comes to self-promotion, consider how far you're willing to go to promote yourself. If you have any blocks about being with people or introducing yourself and generating conversation, or talking about your abilities, then your career is either not going to happen or will be very limited. Consistently putting yourself out there, taking risks, and networking makes a huge difference. I've always loved meeting people and learning about what they do and sharing what I do, so it fits well with self-promotion.

Ultimately, the biggest self-promotion you can do is to deliver the goods in front of the microphone, not to mention getting along well with others involved in the recording session. Consider that you have to choose between two equally talented voice-over artists and one is simply more fun to be around. Which one would you choose?

Networking opportunities arise in many situations outside of your agent. There are events sponsored by SAG and AFTRA (yes, you do want to join), and there are many functions and conferences attended by the directors, producers, casting directors, and TV programmers who potentially could hire you or introduce you to other opportunities. Get to know about these events like your career depends on it. It does.

One surprising thing that's arisen from my voice-over career is teaching. It was probably the furthest thing from my mind as a career or as a way to earn extra money, but it has become important. While I was doing an acting class at Actors Institute in New York, to my surprise the director, Twila Thompson, asked me to develop and teach a voice-over class to expand the school's curriculum. I took it on without hesitation and then set out to learn how to do it by sitting in on different classes of voice-over teachers. What struck me most was that they were just going through the motions and didn't seem to care about the lives they were impacting. I was upset about this because I am very committed to giving and getting value for my and others' time. Teaching to me is a wide-open opportunity to evolve my spirit and advance my knowledge of the craft and the business. This realization has given me the confidence to communicate to strangers the craft that is my life and livelihood.

At first, I demonstrated and trained students in vocal exercises, voice-over technique, and the dynamics of relating to a microphone. I also taught them auditioning techniques and how to navigate the business side of the voice-over industry. But the most interesting and the most powerful learning came from sharing my real-world personal experiences as a working voice-over professional and the methods I used to overcome the most challenging and sometimes devastating experiences. Here's one.

One Friday afternoon, I was jogging in a workout suit back to my apartment after running an errand in downtown Manhattan. I cut through Macy's and ran into an old boyfriend. "Hi Joan-baby," said Thomas. After receiving a friendly hug and updating him that I was now doing voice-overs, he said, "You're not going to believe your timing. The executive producer of *Imus in the Morning* is upstairs to promote their radio show. Go on up!"

Pretending to know who or what *Imus* was, I shook my head yes enthusiastically and headed upstairs. At the area Thomas had directed me to, I found a man alone at a long table putting on his jacket. I asked him if he knew where the *Imus* promotion was.

"Yes, I do, right here," he said, extending his hand. "Hi, I'm Bernard McGuirk, and I'm Executive Producer for *Imus in the Morning*."

"Well, hello," I said. "I'm Joan Baker, and I'm a voice-over artist specializing in character and cartoon voices."

"Really? Well, we happen to be looking for a female who does character voices. Can you get me a tape?"

"Yes, I can," I said. I happened to have one in my waist pack and handed him it. He said he couldn't listen right then because they were packing up to go but asked if I had a card. I gave him one, and he said, "Joan, I'll call you."

Bernard called Monday: "Imus is interested in meeting you for the show, we need you to come down to the radio station." Since I still didn't know who Imus was, I thought it was some rinky-dink station in the boondocks with the call letters I.M.U.S. But I couldn't afford to be picky. They gave me the directions to WFAN, a popular sports' station in Queens.

On the appointed day, the receptionist asked if I had ever met Imus, and when I said no, she said, "Good luck!" As I waited, other employees passing by asked me who I was here to see, and when I said, "Imus," the response was the same: "Oh . . . Good luck." *Who is this guy?* I wondered. Suddenly I heard a commanding male voice over the loud speakers: "Joan Baker, will you please come to Imus's office immediately!" As an employee escorted me down the corridor, other employees signaled me with crossed fingers or cheered, "You can do it" or "Be strong."

A huge seven-foot cutout picture of Imus stood in Imus's entryway. His look was rugged, if not somewhat disheveled, his smile a bit off center, if not something like a growl.

I opened the door, and Imus boomed, "JOAN BAKER!"

I screamed back, "IMUS!"

Imus sat behind his desk like a king on a throne, quickly combing his hair back and forth with one hand and downing water with the other hand. Next to him crooked columns of cassette tapes teetered toward the ceiling. Standing behind him was an emotionless Bernard, and sitting like bookends at opposite ends of the couch were two men whom I recognized: Larry Kenney (who was at my talent agency) and Rob Barlett. Their character voices and impersonations were legendary. Wow, I couldn't believe it!

After twenty minutes of trying to get the tape player started (and we were at a radio station), they finally got the button to work. As it played, I noticed that Imus stopped combing his hair and just listened.

"That was all you?" he said when it was over.

"Yeah," I said.

"We're going to work together," he said and went right back to combing back and forth.

I sat alone silently observing Imus and the voice geniuses reading the script. A paper rustled. A guttural groan. Then a click on Imus's intercom: "God dammit—Charlie! Get your ass in here!" Speakers mounted in every room multiplied his voice exponentially. A chief staff writer scampered into the office, and Imus blasted both the script's and the writer's shortcomings. Then Imus turned his blood-soaked lips to me: "We won't have any time to rehearse—just record."

The shell-shocked writer returned, fed the new script to Imus, and slowly withdrew. Absolute quiet—a short laugh—and then the inevitable "God dammit!" Though humorous, this back-and-forth reordering of the script also nullified any chance of my getting to read the finished script out loud before recording.

"What's so funny?" Imus said to me.

I looked at him, unable to reply, but I was praying that whatever character voice came out of my mouth first would work. The muscles in my face just retained my smile, and I didn't dare say a word. So I dropped my eyes to the script and bit my lip.

"Okay, I'm not your father, so don't expect me to baby you, and if you suck, I'll tell you," he said.

Throughout the recording session, Imus's manner was prickly, and his criticisms flourished, but I was spared his whip, and somehow he was mysteriously likable.

"What's so damn funny?" he moaned again.

My laughter began in response to my nervousness as I flew with whatever voice came out of my mouth, but then I began to feel genuine delight. Somewhere within me I understood how this man's extreme antics of intimidation had charmed the public. He expected people he worked with to cower and fall into line. But when he saw me laugh, he grew confused, intrigued, and was thrown off balance. His demeanor—thank God!—softened, slightly.

"Thank you, Joan. Good job."

Later I learned that he rarely worked with women for very long. People from the office told me they never saw him get along so well with a female, and even one of the geniuses commented on it. They asked what I did. I said I didn't know, but I found him extremely interesting, as I bit my lip.

This experience on the *Imus Show* got me a radio gig on a popular radio program on another station that lasted for six years. It included doing multiple character voices and spoofs, live radio dramas, political satires, interviews with artists, and writing for the show.

It definitely pays to be prepared—even with unlikely people at unlikely places in an unlikely sweaty jogging suit.

Sharing such stories not only helps students understand the business, it helps me come to terms with my path. Teaching, which also includes directing talent in the production of demo reels, took me much deeper into the craft than I had ever imagined and enabled me to discover directing.

If you ask anybody in or out of the entertainment business, they'll tell you that actors must learn to deal with rejection. The word *rejection* has been handed down as if it were something that casting directors, producers, and clients actually do to people. The good news is that it ain't so. In the voice-over industry, voices and their accompanying qualities are selected based on how well they suit the advertiser's specific (and I mean specific) needs. The operative word is not *rejected* but *selected*; voices are chosen. Your voice is either selected or it isn't, but it is never rejected. As you learn about the selection process, you will understand that auditioning truly is a numbers game. Talent sometimes doesn't even enter into it. The talented and not so talented eventually cut through when their voices fit the criteria. This may happen once every twenty-five to fifty auditions or so, though a little more often for the talented.

Okay, with rejection out of the equation, how can voice-over artists deal with not being the One? I focus on my performance, remembering that nailing the audition is one hundred percent with me. I see my responsibility as a talent, and the core question I teach from is how to be my best self in unpredictable situations, to learn to expose vulnerability and risk greatness. I investigate and explore my instrument, train, and study. A no is just a yes waiting to happen. When the yes comes, I'm ready.

Probably the most surprising thing to come out of my involvement in the voice-over industry was meeting the love of my life. It was on his birthday, and he was a promo writer/producer for ABC News who hired me after listening to my demo. But here's the clincher. It was his receptionist, whom I had befriended a few days before, who after overhearing him talking about the possibility of hiring a woman voice-over (something ABC News hadn't done for about seven years) yelled, "I put Joan Baker's demo reel on your desk yesterday. Why don't you listen to it?" He did, he called, and the rest is our future.

Another incredible thing that has come out of working in voice-over is that I have honed my marketing skills and ability to communicate effectively. As a result, I've been able to partner with my husband in forming and building an ad agency we currently operate in New York City.

I'd like my voice to be remembered as one that inspires and motivates people, to be remembered as a vital instrument of transformation. One evening I sat alone with my father when he was in the latter stages of Alzheimer's; he was completely unable to speak or communicate in any way. Even still, I was able to sense his voice through who I knew him to be as a father and a human being. His spirit was totally communicating. So if I had to live my life without the ability to verbally communicate, I believe I would ground myself in my spirit that I have always trusted and continue to be the best human being I could be.

5th SECRET

Don't hold yourself back. Learn to bare your vulnerability and to reach out and risk being great. Think of it as showing up for work at your best.

Fred Collins

Fred Collins is the voice of *ABC News*. His was the first voice heard on color television, and in the course of his career, he has been the spokesman for over 300 of the Fortune 500 companies.

WHEN I WAS VERY YOUNG, I RECEIVED A CHECK FOR ONE DOLLAR FOR saying, "Dad, are you going to get a vacation this year?" An older actor playing my father answered, "Yes, son, why?" And I responded, "Let's go to Michigan!" When I cashed that check for one dollar, I knew what I wanted to do for the rest of my life!

There were no obstacles to overcome because there were so few kids my age doing radio. As I grew older, I just automatically rose to the next level of trying to keep up with the kind of vocal delivery being bought.

Fortunately, while on the announcing staff at NBC, I became quite busy doing class A network commercials. When my then agent, Charles Tranum, suggested that I prepare a demo tape, I took a stack of twenty-three commercials that were currently running to my friend Bob Verno at his studio, Judrac Productions. At that time, demo reels consisted of full thirty and sixty-second commercials. My friend Bob looked at the stack of commercials and said (as only he would say it), "What makes you think any fucking casting director is going to listen to twenty-three fucking commercials?" Then he directed me to leave the spots, and he would see what he could do. What he did was to create the very first voice-over demo of its kind. Bob not only used snippets of each of the twenty-three commercials, but he put them in a humorous arrangement that totaled two minutes and seventeen seconds.

Until ICM (International Creative Management), I was always approached by the agent, not the other way around. Why did agents want me? In my case, it was because they heard me on the NBC radio/TV network. However, someone starting out should always assemble a voice-over commercial/promo CD. There are many studios that can supply proper copy and background music. When making an appointment with a recognized agent, mention that you have a voice-over CD or that you're perfectly willing to read live for them.

Always be on time. Be especially pleasant with receptionists. Never ever knock or make fun of the copy—unless the producer does, and the writer isn't present! One secret move (and only if you are established) is: *Never give your best read on the first take!* This gives the director or producer or casting director the opportunity to give direction—and, on the second take, demonstrates that you take great direction! When reading for a novice, or a "bad taste director," you can still do the first take a little "off." Then say to the director, "I didn't feel right about that reading. How would *you* suggest I approach this copy?"

As a result of doing a favor for a client of mine, I was asked by him if I would mind making a gag birthday recording for his friend's wife. I assumed when the client and his friend showed up at the studio that they were both from the same agency. A few days later, I received a letter from one of the larger advertising agencies in New York. I had never worked for this agency and was surprised when I opened it to find a thank you note from the gentleman for whose wife we had made the recording. Then I couldn't help but notice that his title was Senior Vice President! A few days later, he called to tell me that I would be the spokesman for his biggest account at the agency! At the first session, my newfound friend introduced me to the lady director (who also was the vice president casting director at the agency). When I went into the studio, I asked the engineer I knew if he would mind switching the Telefunken mike (that in those days was used primarily for music) for an RCA 77d. At this point, the very upset lady director hit the talkback button and said, "Why don't you let the engineer do his job! He knows his mikes better than you do!" For the rest of the session, she tried very hard to make me look bad. To make a much longer story shorter, here is what happened. Later that day, I discovered that the lady was also the head casting director at the agency and that she had not been consulted when I replaced the other spokesman. That afternoon I called the agency and asked to speak with her. When she asked what I wanted, I told her how surprised I was that the vice president had given me the job because of the birthday gag. I quickly added that if I was in her position, and a vice president had hired someone without asking me, "I would hate me even more than you do." As a result of that call and the apology, the lady casting director hired me as spokesman for many of that agency's largest accounts!

About smoking. At the time, I couldn't read copy with confidence without inhaling a cigarette and I was smoking between five and a half and six packs a day. My suits were made with a special pocket that held two packs of More regular and menthol cigarettes. Though normally a pussycat, if any actor asked me to put out the cigarette, I'd tell him or her to leave the studio until I finished my read. I was literally a nicotine addict. I haven't smoked a cigarette since I was told by my cardiologist to put it out at his office at 10:30 AM, December 31, 1984, because I was having a heart attack right then.

The big heart attack came while I was in intensive care at Mt. Sinai hospital at 3:30 AM January 1, 1985. When I was finally in my room at the hospital, the doctor in charge of the post-cardiac department, Dr. S. R. Levine (husband of Mary Tyler Moore), said to me "Mr. Collins, you realize that we can't guarantee a great deal in medicine." I replied, "Of course." Then Dr. Levine said, "In your case, we're going to make an exception. We are willing to give you a guarantee *in writing* that if you go back to smoking, you will have a fatal heart attack in six months. And if you live seven months, you can sue us!"

The blessing of all this is that in addition to the health factor, my vocal range has increased over a full octave.

Rejection used to be a given in a voice-over career. Assumptions for rejection are many, and in most cases have little to do with the talent of the voice-over. Reasons range from age, looks, manner of dress, general attitude in the audition, hair color or lack of hair, to the mood of the casting person before the audition. The main defense against that feeling of rejection is not to question one's own talent and abilities but to accept the vagaries of the system.

When I started in New York, I was too naïve (coming from Fort Wayne, Indiana) to realize that rejection *wasn't* an essential part of auditioning. Realistically, with so many voice-overs competing for even the smallest job today, the feeling of rejection doesn't exist anymore. No experienced professional going to an audition expects to be chosen for the job. The word *rejection* is replaced by the word *elation* on those *rare* occasions when one wins the audition. Another reason for going to an audition is to meet and visit with old friends!

Analyzing copy is strictly an individual thing. The first step in any case is, hopefully, to get an idea of the intent of the writer or client as to the personality of the copy. Many times, even when the desired vocal approach is described, it turns out *not* to be what the client wants to hear. There's no set process for analyzing copy, because there are so many variables. For instance, one piece may appear to be written as hard sell, but it should be read in a soft sell manner. My own approach has always been to look at the copy and to try to impart through my voice the values of certain words, and to try to bring those meanings into the ear of the listener.

I've never learned anything about how my general psyche impacts my ability to succeed in voice-overs. I go to an audition, visit with old friends in the business, do the audition, engage in pleasant conversation, go to the next one, go home, and usually forget the names of the products for which I auditioned.

Personal obstacles have *never* impacted my professional path. My career being enhanced by humility, I offer the following story. When I was quite young and acting on stage, I was blessed with eidetic imagery. During early rehearsals, I easily memorized every actor's lines as well as my own. During dress rehearsal, the director, Reid Erikson, gave a rather strong critique to everyone in the cast—except me. I asked Mr. Erikson if he had any directional suggestions for me. At this point, in the presence of the whole cast, he said, in a rather loud voice, "The rest of them, I still have *some hope for!*" To this day, when I do a take, and the director has no suggestions for me, my mind still does a flashback to Reid Erikson's comment, and I wonder if this director has given up on getting the right reading out of me!

How do I find work? Before, advertising agencies called my agent for my services. Most of those who called are either retired or are no longer with us. Now, almost all of my work comes through the efforts of my agents at ICM. I'm fortunate to have a state of the art ISDN system in my apartment, with the same complimentary equipment plus an even better microphone than is used at the networks. This provides me with networking abilities not generally available to someone starting out on a voice-over career. There are all sorts of gimmicks available today for those just beginning. Even agents who send out CDs with all their clients every year use them. Some voice-overs create a voice-mail demo and then distribute it to advertising agencies, casting companies, and studios. There are also note pads, pens, note-size and CD demos. They all have the artist's name, company, voice mail number, and agent's name and number. Some beginning voice-over talents have done well using this method. Unfortunately, it also requires no small investment of money, time, and effort.

Through the years, my work as a voice-over artist has allowed me a comfortable way of life and an opportunity to meet an extraordinary number of talented, gracious, charming, generous, and devoted people, some of whom I can truly call loving friends.

If a working voice-over isn't working enough to make ends meet, then he or she should consider the following. First, try to get an honest evaluation of your talent from a recognized successful agent. If there is absolutely no encouragement there, then give it up and seek other possibilities for making a decent living. If you're assured that you have the talent to continue, then by all means seek out the best agents and try to sign with them. In these days, it's almost impossible to make it big without an agent.

My career in voice-overs has been everything I always thought it would be. Just think about it for a moment. Unless you seek fame (which I personally would have great difficulty accepting), concentrate on all the advantages: no need for costume, makeup, memorizing, having to be available for eight hours for one on-camera commercial when you might be able to do half a dozen off-camera commercials in an hour or two. What more could one expect out of a well paying career with so little effort?

I suppose I'd like my voice to be remembered, but mostly I want to be remembered as a very decent person who happened to be blessed with a good voice, who used it in many different ways, some of which were for very good causes such as recording for the blind and dyslexic. I can't imagine my life without a voice—without the ability to verbally or coherently communicate. But then, I diligently concentrate on all the amazing things I am blessed with in life: being able to walk, talk, breathe, see, smell, taste, think, remember, love, and be loved by my wife and children and true friends. It pains me to recognize that I have relatives and friends suffering with Alzheimer's whose blessings are taken from them, one after another, until there is a room "without."

6th SECRET

Rejection? No experienced professional going to *an* audition expects to be chosen for the job. The word *rejection* is replaced by the word *elation* on those *rare* occasions when one wins the audition.

Janice Pendarvis

Janice Pendarvis has acquired voice-over credits for Exxon, Jaguar, Kool-Aid, McDonald's, and Burger King, and her voice can be heard on TV promos with such clients as Disney, WNET-13, and FOX News.

IT HAS TAKEN TIME, PATIENCE, AND WORK FOR ME TO DEVELOP INTO A working voice actor and announcer. As I learned more about the art and craft of voice-overs, and as the industry learned to trust my talent, my career developed gradually. During this process, I've had to have a lot of patience with myself and with the industry; I still need to have this patience. Most important to the process of becoming a working voice talent has been just jumping in and doing it. That's the best way for me to learn.

I'm also a singer, and I've worked as a lead and as a background singer with a diverse roster of artists: Sting, Philip Glass, Laurie Anderson, Peter

Tosh, Roberta Flack, Luiz Bonfa, and others. I started in commercials as a jingle singer and often was the singer who was asked to read the copy in the donut. My friend actor-writer-singer David Smeryl knew I was doing a voice-over here and there, so he put me in touch with a friend of his, Janice Scott, who did commercials for Columbia Records. I started doing voice-overs for her, and she finally said to me, "You know, you should do this for real." She suggested I make up a tape, she would make a list of the best commercial agents in New York, and we would work our way down the list. I started listening to commercials on TV, taping the sound of the spots I thought were best suited for me onto a handheld cassette recorder. Then I wrote down the copy from those spots and practiced reading them with the same cassette recorder until I liked what I was doing. I went into the studio and made a demo using the copy I had taken from the TV spots. When the demo was completed, Janice Scott called the first and the best voice-over agent on the list—Cunningham, Escott, Slevin & Dipene (CESD)—to tell them that I would be sending a tape and that she had worked with me and was recommending me to them. I sent my demo to them, they signed me, and I've been with CESD ever since.

To be perfectly honest, I haven't done a lot of self-promotion. Since so much of my work was singing in the early years of my voice-over career, I was able to concentrate on being good at the voice-over jobs I got and enjoying them as opposed to promoting myself. I think my low-key approach has worked well for me. I do an amazingly great job when I'm called. Employers remember that and call again. My point of view when I have done self-promotion is that I am certainly one of the best at what I do. I love doing it with a passion. I've got a great range. Working with me is easy, enjoyable, fast, and hassle-free. If you're looking for a voice, then you should call me.

A long time ago I went to an audition at a major agency. There were no more than two other women waiting when I arrived. The other women were both white. I sat down and started studying the copy. After a while, I noticed the head of casting kept coming out, looking at the sign-in sheet, looking around the waiting area, and then leaving again. I waited for at least half an hour after the other women had been seen. Finally, he came out and said to the receptionist, "Did you see Janice Pendarvis? I see that she signed in a while ago, but where is she? The receptionist turned several shades of red and softly said to him, while pointing at me, "She's been sitting right there all the time!" Suddenly I felt like the invisible man Ralph Ellison talked about. There's no worse feeling than knowing that your brown skin makes you nonexistent to the person you have to deal with. There was no intentional malice shown; my presence was simply irrelevant. This was one helluva bad feeling to carry into an audition. As bad as I felt, I knew that he was the one with the problem, not me. Not wanting his problem to be mine, I reached down deep and let go of the terrible feeling I had. He apologized for keeping me waiting. We did the audition, and he timed me with a stopwatch. After my first read, he looked surprised and said, "That was a very intelligent read. Can you take one second off?"

Smiling, I replied, "Sure!" I cut exactly one second. He looked even more surprised.

"Gee, you took off exactly a second. Can you take off another second?"

"I think so," I replied. I took off another second. He smiled and complimented me on my skills. I smiled, thanked him for the audition, and left.

At this point in my career, rejection has little impact on me emotionally because I don't take it personally. If you take every rejection in this business personally, you'll go crazy. For instance, when you don't get the job you auditioned for, that could be considered a form of rejection. However, I've learned to enjoy each audition for its own sake. If I get the job, great, if I don't, that's okay, too. Rejection used to bother me a lot. I would hear a spot I auditioned for and didn't get and be really annoyed if the spot had lousy voice-over talent or a totally different direction than the casting person insisted I follow in my audition. Now I just make a mental note of it and continue my day. It used to bother me to hear something that I knew I was right for but didn't get a call to audition. Now I make a plan to investigate how I can be seen for that account in the future or I forget about it.

My process for working on copy has developed over time using patience and practice. First, I decide where I'm going to pitch my voice: high, medium, or low, based on the traits of the character I have to portray. Then I read the copy to myself several times to find the rhythm and timing of how I want to read it. I often look for more than one way to read a commercial so I have alternatives in mind for the client. The process is very internal for me and more instinctual than conscious at this point. I look for the important points and meaningful moments and work them! If I'm doing a cold reading, I just go for it since I can always find a flow and I'm really good at looking ahead. I learned a lot about reading copy in the early years of my career from a director named Lou DeCharme. I booked the first job I ever auditioned for through CESD. Howard Rollins was the other actor on the job, and Lou DeCharme directed. Lou is brilliant at going beyond telling you what to do because he shows you how to get there. I use everything I ever learned from him every time I work. I love Lou for giving me some really precious tools and insight into my craft. There is no greater gift.

It has been said of obstacles that whatever doesn't kill you makes you stronger. I guess I must be pretty strong right now because I'm still here. Women get much less voice-over work than men; black folks get less voice-over work than white folks. Black women—well there aren't a lot of us in the voice-over club. I don't look at these realities as personal obstacles; they are built-in systemic obstacles I have no control over. But I do have control over how I deal with them. I have control over my attitude and feelings. I have learned not to go on other people's trips when I'm working. I come to the job happy and I leave happy no matter what! A large part of my success is having overcome the desire to react to what I perceive as negative stimuli. I stay focused strictly on the job at hand and on being happy every moment of my life.

I believe that race and gender have limited my success, but I deal with those barriers and work extra hard to get more than just the obvious calls. Thank God for the African American market. It gives black talent a place to exist and practice our craft when the rest of the world isn't interested in us. I cherish doing black spots even though the so-called generic spots often pay more. I love doing the generic thing, too. Both are natural to me; I am black and American, and I do excellent work in both worlds. The barriers might slow me down, but they can't stop me. It ain't over till it's over; there's a lot more for me to do in the world of voice-overs.

In the beginning of my career, I found voice-over work through the jingle houses I sang for as well as through my agent. Now I find commercials, promo work, and some industrials through my agent. I find film looping jobs and the occasional industrial on my own. My work as a voice-over artist has had an unexpected effect on my skills as a singer. I get into the text of a song on a whole new level and have much more focus and intensity. There is so much more depth to my singing performances now.

I also find that my phone skills have become really intense! Sometimes I feel like the Bene Gesserit in the science fiction novel *Dune*, who used "The Voice" to influence others. It's kinda funny. When people ask how to break into voice-overs, I usually tell them how I did it to show that anything is possible. Who would think that you could send out one copy of the first voice-over tape you ever made and get signed to a top agent? Study the field, determine if you really have a shot at it, make a tape, and go for it. Be patient; don't give up. I think sometimes folks just want to see if you're serious enough about this career to stick around. Most of all, enjoy it for what it is. A voice-over career has got to be more than a stepping stone on your way to fame and fortune in film, TV, or onstage. If it isn't, your disdain for all of us who really love this will make you unpleasant to work with and taint your work, and you won't be around long.

I want my voice to be remembered as a unique instrument savored for its warmth, richness, accessibility, and wide range of possibilities, whether speaking or singing. Remember me as Janice Pendarvis—Professional Voice. Remember that my instrument expressed every day reality and fantasy, elegance and raw emotion, sensuality and grace, innocence and sexuality. Remember that I loved every second of doing it. From time to time when I've been sick or really tired and had to sing, I've had to do vocal silence and not talk or utter a sound for a few days. It is so hard to be relegated to a pad and pencil. People treated me like I couldn't hear or was stupid just because I couldn't talk. Even people that knew me changed how they treated me. The pad and pencil became like a cool drink of water for me, stranded in the desert of not having a voice. Pad and pencil was the only way I had to communicate. Fortunately therapeutic vocal silences don't last forever. If I had no voice and no coherent way to communicate, it would be like being sentenced to solitary confinement for life without a chance of parole, a horrible, sad, and lonely fate indeed.

7th SECRET

Brace yourself. No matter how physically sick, emotionally upset, or self-doubting you may feel, the thespian credo requires you to turn in a stellar performance when you step in front of the microphone.

Les Marshak

Les Marshak is the voice of the Macy's commercials and NBC Sports. He has announced the Academy Awards, as well as many other Network Award Shows, including the Emmys, SAG Awards, Grammys, and, for twenty-one consecutive years, Broadway's Tony Awards. He has introduced the President of the U.S. yearly on numerous specials from Washington, D.C., going back to Ronald Reagan.

RADIO AND TV WERE PASSIONS OF MINE SINCE CHILDHOOD. DURING THE 1950s, I attended many live radio and TV shows and fantasized about becoming an announcer. From the early days of Buffalo Bob Smith and the *Howdy Doody Show* to the legendary baseball play-by-play announcers—especially Mel Allen—I was mesmerized. I loved to impersonate them all. So, in the spring of 1961, when I heard about the WABC Star Search, I jumped right in. I was a sophomore student majoring in pharmacy at Columbia University and I wasn't thrilled with making suppositories and nearly blowing up the organic chemistry lab.

The Star Search began as a WABC promotion whereby listeners could watch for a mobile unit to visit their neighborhood and then audition. That for some reason didn't work out for the station. So, they invited listeners to send in a postcard if they were interested in auditioning in the DJ, musician, or singer category. My card was one of about a thousand selected. Auditions were scheduled at the ABC Television Studio on West 66th Street. They involved a couple of pages of commercial and promotional copy with some ad libbing. I gave it my best shot and was a wreck for the next few weeks waiting for the announcement. Then I received a telegram (remember those?) stating that I was one of twelve finalists with an interview scheduled. After the interview, the heart pounding really began. No news, no word at all for a few weeks. Then on a weeknight in July a phone call came from a man with a gravelly voice. He said he was Scott Muni. But how did I know it wasn't one of my fanatic radio buddies calling with a Muni impersonation? I played it cool. It really was Scott (already a major radio star in New York radio). And there I was, on the air, hearing that I'd won the Star Search. When the dust settled, and more telegrams arrived from family and friends, I found myself living a schizoid life of pharmacy student during the week—and radio "star"(?) on the weekend. My first on-air assignment was a live broadcast with Muni from Freedomland Amusement Park in the Bronx. It was a most surreal experience. I assisted Scott on the air for a few months. Then Bruce Morrow, a.k.a. Cousin Brucie, a young legend already, was hired. He took a liking to me and put me to work on his show reporting high school football and basketball scores and live appearances at Palisades Amusement Park. Ironically, years later, he would marry my wife's best friend, Jodie, and we all became very close.

Pounding the pavement in search of voice-over jobs was tedious early on. Your calling card is your demo tape, which is expected to feature highlights of your best work. However, if you're a voice-over virgin, what do you put on your reel? You need to create dummy commercials. Here's how I did it. I'd record a few hours of primetime TV on my VCR, then sift through all the ads and promos to find material comfortable for me to voice. I would re-create a few ads in a studio with some production music, and—voila!—my tape. It helps if you're doing work at a radio station or have an engineer buddy at a recording studio to cut costs. Then, when you start getting hot and your stuff starts hitting the airwaves, you, of course, have to go back and revise, and revise, and revise your demo. Keeping the length of the demo to no more than a couple of minutes was always a challenge. The cat food spot and the airline spot are so great, but so similar in style—so which one gets deleted?

The digital world has made constructing demo tapes a breeze. In the old analog days, your demo would become outdated in no time, and the whole industry would have possession of it. So, how would you get them to destroy the old for the new? Now your demo is available on your agent's website and can be easily updated in a studio and reassembled on the Web for all to peruse. Another frustration is "When is a spot that you've voiced too outdated?" You've heard the line, "You're only as good as your last film (or spot)." Realistically, you're as good as your best spot, even though producers and agents might think it dated.

I realized early on in my voice-over career that too much reliance on my agent(s) is not the best professional strategy to grow my business. An agent is an indispensable part of the teamwork that you create. You need to be seen and heard by the industry, and a good agent has the means to make that happen. I found that developing a good personal rapport with a producer, writer, studio engineer, and so forth is a way of planting seeds for the future. Creative directors and producers move around the industry a great deal and feel most comfortable booking someone with whom they're familiar. After you've booked an enjoyable and hopefully lucrative session, sending flowers, remembering a birthday, or taking the producer to lunch can only work in your favor.

Three assignments stand out because of their strangeness or stress factor. I was booked on a Cruex (jock itch) radio spot as a jogger running on a track. Looking for authenticity, they required me to run in place while delivering my lines. They had me run in place with a mike placed near my feet to pick up the sounds of feet pounding on a wet track. I was in decent physical shape, so I had to run in place for over twenty minutes to achieve the out-of-breath delivery they wanted. How silly I felt at first, running alone in a soundproof studio on a wet plastic floor!

Another experience taught me the need for total focus when doing voice-over work. As announcer on the live Tony Awards telecast, I was usually situated in either a dressing room or some abandoned storage room with my mike, headphones, and TV monitor. Before the telecast moved to Radio City Music Hall, legitimate Broadway theatres were the site. Some were smaller with fewer available rooms. The year the show originated from the Lunt-Fontanne, I was literally up in the rafters. They put me in a room on the top floor of this ancient theatre where the lighting guys would take a break and use the toilet. There were lots of live-announce cues on this show, and a few times I had to overcome a lighting technician flushing the toilet ten feet from me.

Focus! Focus! Focus! The assignment that required the most intense focus was my initial experience in Los Angeles announcing the Academy Awards telecast. Focus and raw fear! A live show seen and heard by over a billion people worldwide. Just thinking about what I needed to do during the most intense opening ten minutes of the show caused many sleepless nights and wild nightmares prior to the event. Every Oscar telecast begins with the traditional arrivals. An hour or so prior to airtime, a separate platoon of producers, writers, and cameramen tape the celebrities walking the red carpet. Then they edit with no more than four or five seconds for each star. Copy is quickly put together on individual index cards for me to read. They conclude this process only a few minutes before airtime. I'm given just one run-through with the index cards and then whisked into the theatre to be at my station for the live show. On cue, I read the cards synching each one with the actor or actresses on the screen. Again, I have no more than four seconds for each cut. This goes on for ten minutes. Falling behind is like watching a set of dominos collapse. Focus and breathe. Focus and breathe. At the end of the arrivals, before I have to introduce Whoopie Goldberg or Billy Crystal, I cut my mike and scream.

When I was growing up listening to the radio, some voices really connected with me. What quality did they have? I learned in my own professional work that I could obtain that quality by isolating one individual and talking to him or her as if that person were with me in the booth. Many producers have directed me by saying, "Tell me a story." It's amazing how the act of personalizing your words results in the message getting through. Taking basic acting lessons helped me focus on interpreting copy rather than listening to my voice.

Just as a musician interprets the work of a composer, I take the words of a copywriter and try to find the essence of what he or she is trying to communicate. The ultimate compliment from a writer is that I've nailed it—that my interpretation of the copy is exactly what was in that writer's mind. This is one of the ways I'd like my voice to be remembered. In addition, I'd like it to be remembered as one that was flexible and adaptable to many genres and demographic groups. After all, I'm straddling two centuries.

If I ever lost the ability to communicate, I would hope to be surrounded by people who understood me and cared about me enough to be able to express what I could not.

8th SECRET

An agent is an indispensable collaborator in the creation of your career. However, developing a good personal rapport with producers, writers, and studio engineers with whom you work directly is an effective way of planting seeds for future work.

George DelHoyo

George DelHoyo has been the primary voice for the FOX Television Network for over five years. He also has voiced the promotional campaigns of over 500 feature films, including *A Beautiful Mind,* which won the Academy Award for Best Picture, as well as many campaigns for the HBO Television Network. These include *The Sopranos* and *Six Feet Under.* He also has been the voice of hundreds of commercials on television and radio for products such as The New York Stock Exchange and Honda.

I CAME TO THE VOICE-OVER PROFESSION FROM ACTING, SO IT WAS EVERYTHING I did as an actor that ultimately brought me to this facet of the industry. Todd Sussman, a good friend and a well-known character actor who was doing voice-overs, kept telling me I had to try it, but I was very skeptical because it seemed like there were only *six* people doing it! I definitely thought of it as exclusive in the sense that not that many people got to do it. In fact, I thought it was an even rarer group than that of successful actors because that is what I'd been told, and there was evidence of that from everything I heard on the air. *What are the odds?* I thought. It was daunting. But Todd was so relentless that now I'm eternally grateful to him.

Every time we had lunch, he said, "When are you going to do it? When are you going to try?"

"Oh, come on," I said. "I don't see that as a possibility."

And then, finally, I said, "Just give me the name of somebody that'll do a demo."

And he said, "Great, go see this guy."

"I'll just tell you one thing, Todd," I said. "I just want to get one job to pay for this demo. That's all I want."

So I went to see Nick Omana here in town. He teaches classes and workshops for beginners, intermediate, and advanced voice-over talent. Plus, he does demos. There aren't many people in L.A. who do that. But Nick is very decent and a man of integrity. When I met him, he said, "Well, read this copy." And so I read a couple of pieces of copy. And he could have easily, in a rather self-serving way, said, "You need to take my intermediate course" or something and made some money off of me, but he was very straight and honest. Instead, he said, "You know, I think that you're ready to go. We just need to get you out there and do a demo, because you are ready. And he also said something very kind and encouraging. He said, "And I predict you're going to work a lot."

I said, "Really?"

He said, "Absolutely."

And, by the way, Nick does voice-overs.

So I did the demo, and this is after I'd been working as an actor for twenty-five years. I've worked on Broadway, and Off Broadway, and on national tours; I've worked in regional theater. I've done several TV series and films. I started in New York and did a couple of shows there in the seventies. I came to Los Angeles in '78 when I got signed as a contract player for Universal Studios. There I started working on-camera in all venues, from episodic to movies of the week, from sitcoms to soaps.

I've been fortunate to gather a lot of experience over the years, and it's all tied up in what I do now, no matter how small, or how seemingly insignificant the spot or the piece I'm recording. I've thought about it. It's not an unexamined thing I'm talking about. However absurd that little spot may seem or sound, I know that everything I've ever done and learned on stage, and everywhere I've ever been, and everything that's been taught to me by my teachers is all a part of what I'm offering now. It's a good and interesting thing to note about one's self. We are a product of the path we've walked and the people we've encountered along the way.

Eventually I made my first demo tape. Making the tape was the easiest part. You can get any decent engineer to make a tape for you. I thought it was good at the time. What did I know? I did a variety of voices and characters, an old man, accents, dialects, all kinds of stuff. There were a couple of voices that were pretty straightforward, but most of it was animated voices and different things. They weren't bad, but they weren't what would get you work . . . or an agent. For the most part, if the client wants an old man, they're going to get an old man. Truth be told, my tape was all over the map. I was offering too many colors, I guess, in my naïve way. Listening to it now, I notice probably two spots that I would say pinpoint the beginning of my sound, what I turned into. There's the hint of what was to come.

I started sending my tape to voice-over agents. I didn't send it to many because I didn't know many, but on the recommendation, again, of my friend Todd, I sent it to his agent at Sutton, Barth & Vennari, a premier agency. They passed, said they weren't interested. "We have 'that sound' already," they said. "Although he sounds good, and we like this sound, we don't really need it right now." Of course, I thought maybe this was just a nice way of rejecting me. The woman who owns the agency, Rita Vennari, is just great. And she has been gracious enough to say to me years later, "What a mistake, of all the silly things I've ever done." Believe me, if I wasn't with another agent, I would be with her; she's one of the *best!*

Then I sent my tape to the Tisherman Agency because, again, my friend Todd knew Steve, the owner. I sent it there with a cover letter saying that Todd was my friend and an inspiration to me. My tape, picture, and résumé ended up in the garbage. Luckily Nancy Simon, an agent who's no longer there but just the dearest person, saw the picture languishing in the garbage can. And she said, "Wait a minute! I know this guy." She pulled it out and said, "Oh, this is George Deloy!" (That was the name I had at the time. Now it's DelHoyo, which is my birth and legal name.) She said, "I know this guy, and he's a nice guy and a good actor." Thankfully, she had a fond memory of me. She listened to the tape and then asked Steve

Tisherman to listen to it. When he did, he had the same reaction as Rita, and he's another top agent. Nancy said, "No, you should sign him, because he speaks Spanish." (I had a little snippet of Spanish on it.) Nancy then called me and said, "We want to sign you, and, frankly, it wasn't that easy of a sell, but you speak Spanish." This was over thirteen years ago.

The idea was that I was going to do Spanish. But, of course, I speak fluent English and have done 99 percent of my work as an actor in English. So they started to send me out on English auditions, and for whatever reason—luck, or the stars aligning, or whatever you want to call it—I got three of the first four they sent me to.

The first time I went into an audition, I was there with all these tremendous voices that you'd recognize. I could hear them auditioning through the door and I thought, "Aw, man, those guys are great. What am I going to do in there? I can't do that!" But I just went in there and did whatever I did, and like I say, there was good fortune, good luck, or maybe, just the good grace of God. I managed to get these three out of the first four auditions, which I thought was pretty cool. But my agents thought, "Wow, that's pretty amazing!"

I think that Steve and everybody sat up and took notice and said, hey, let's pay some attention and really push this guy. Of course, just getting an agent was the most amazing hurdle. But my story *after* getting an agent is not one of those "It was so hard, I didn't get any work, and I starved, and I didn't know how to do it, but I got better and better" stories. It's not that way at all. I hit the ground absolutely running—sprinting, almost. Within the first year, I had increased my income a lot, and then the second year it grew and grew, and it's been an exponential growth from that day forth. I can't explain it. Other than the old saying that—as somebody rather brilliantly put it—"Luck is when opportunity meets preparation." I think my situation proves that to be true. And, it's the only explanation I can come up with. The only way I can figure it out is that I was just ready. I was also fortunate to be in a time when advertising was beginning to shift toward a more American conversational mode of communication, as opposed to a kind of omnipotent voice, or a voice of God, a voice of authority. So I was fortunate in that.

Other than being known to my parents, my wife and kids—those who love me—I would like to be known in the industry as somebody who is really a professional and easy to work with because of what I brought to the table, in terms of a willingness to take direction, a spirit of collaboration and patience. I believe that when you're working, it's a mistake to feel, well, "I'm the Talent!" "I'm the Voice!" The reality is, as I say to the people who mix my voice, on any given spot I'm only as good as the mixer.

A mixer can make me sound like I have a cleft palate or I'm sibilant or I can't pronounce words. A good mixer makes you sound great! It's also not just the mixer, it's the producer, it's the editor, it's everybody involved. So you're just a part, a piece of a larger picture. The minute you start thinking you're the piece, you're really wrong, because when you get there, it's all about how do we make this thing the best possible product we can. That requires everyone involved, and so my respect goes out to all of the people I'm working with because I'm so dependent on them. Above all, I'm dependent upon my primary agent at the Tisherman Agency, Vanessa Gilbert. Without her encouragement, professionalism, and tireless efforts on my behalf, I could not begin to do what I do.

I think if I've learned anything over the years, it's that there are human lessons about our lives and behavior that affect our work in every way because we *are* the work! We are the canvas. We are the product that we are ultimately trying to sell. That simple truism bleeds into every aspect of our business. Remember that since you are the product, you should make yourself the *best* product you can be. And that is not just in your preparation as far as schooling and instruction; it's your experiences, in your daily life.

You can't be any more truthful than you are in life. And, since truth is what we're trying to say, even if you're selling the most absurd product in the most absurd situation, an element of truth has to be there, and you have to believe it, and you have to be enthusiastic, and it has to be a part of you, and you have to get behind it. Even the most untrained ear can discern the subtlety of that truth. It's just absorbed as: This is true, and this isn't. We must bring that truth to everything we do. No matter how silly or absurd it may seem. If you don't believe it, they won't believe it. If you don't want to buy it, if you don't want to see it, if you don't want to own it or get it or go do it, then they won't either. The authentic you is what's needed. Don't be anything you're not. You can't be anything more than what you are. You can certainly be *less* than what you are, which is what most people end up doing when they try so hard to be something other than themselves. But you can only be fully what you are. The trick is to find that out, and that's the hardest thing.

I think that most of us struggle for years trying to be something other, better, greater, different from what we are. And it's a logical thing. You're trying to please. You want to be what they want. "Oh, *that's* what they want. They want me to be like *that*, like *him*, like *her! Sound* like that. *Look* like that!" But that's a loser's game. And it's only in finding out what you are, and bringing that to it, that you succeed, because you can't be more or different than what you are, you see? And so we waste our time. But once you find your voice—what you are—then you bring something different and unique to the game, and that's what people respond to. So for whatever reason—maybe it was just maturity and all that experience—but I finally got to the point where I could walk in and say, "What those guys are bringing is great. And I can't bring what they're bringing, but I could bring you this, and it's what I am." People responded to that.

Keep in mind, too, that your relationships with people are important. A testament to that is the fact that somebody picked my picture out of a garbage can because she remembered me positively. What if I had ignored that person in our dealings years ago, or been perfunctory, or just not ever really dealt with her or considered her? Fortunately, I didn't. I was inclusive in my behavior towards her, and she remembered me positively. It's important that we are kind to other people and considerate and patient. I've had this experience many times where people have come back after ten years, twelve or fifteen years, and remembered me: We met this day, and blah-blah-blah, and you said . . . They start to reminisce, and it's always worked out in my favor, because I believe everybody deserves to be considered. We want to be considered.

Oddly enough, all this comes full circle, because what I'm talking about affects what your product is. It affects who you are, and what you bring to it, and what you give, and what your voice is, and the authenticity of that. So it's all a part of the same thing.

I don't think about how my voice will be remembered or how even my work will be remembered. I think about how I will be remembered as a person. I hope my voice is remembered as authentic.

The thought of living out my last years in basic silence, observing the world from within, would be painful beyond description. I would hope to be able to communicate in other ways, although I don't know that a person with Alzheimer's always can. It's really about losing the ability to communicate in all those ways you are familiar with, be it writing or speaking, signing or gesturing. Maybe, finally, you can only "speak" with your eyes . . . and then even that way is closed to you. That's a very profound thing. I can't imagine it any more than I can imagine my life without sight or hearing.

All those things are so important to what I do. I gesticulate a lot. I sometimes joke that the problem would be not losing my voice, but losing my arms. I orchestrate when I speak, I use my whole body in my communication. I envision the words; I place them in the air with my hands. I point to places, I draw things in, I'm like a windmill, and I'm always moving my arms. I hit things. I actually hit my knuckles all the time. I joke, oh man, this is such a dangerous business, and other people respond, "My gosh, how would you do your work if you didn't have your arms?"

9th SECRET

Don't try to be something you're not, and you may not even know you're trying. The real you is what they want. The trick is to find your authentic voice and own it, be it.

Valerie Smaldone

Valerie Smaldone is a successful voice-over artist who has recorded over 1,000 promos (NBC News, Cinemax, CBS, HBO), radio and TV spots (Publix Supermarkets, Minute Maid, Easy Spirit, Lifetime Television), and video news releases (Victoria's Secret, Doral Spa). A five-time *Billboard Magazine* Personality of the Year award winner, she is best known for her unprecedented success holding the #1 position in the New York radio market and the nation as mid-day host of 106.7 Lite-FM NYC.

I'VE BEEN WORKING AT VOICE-OVERS SINCE MY COLLEGE DAYS WHEN I SAW A notice on the bulletin board of my university station, WFUV, requesting college students to voice a show for, well, other college students. I called, got hired, and received my first paycheck for $25. I photocopied the check because it was a monumental feat to me.

I never studied voice-over technique and I never studied radio technique. I am the poster child for on-the-job training. And train I did. For four years during college, I worked on every radio show possible, often-times sleeping on the floor of the station. I seemed to be a natural because I was a very good cold reader, and for that I credit my mother. As a child, when I absolutely refused to attend kindergarten, my mother, who was a schoolteacher, was mortified. A compromise was negotiated when she said I would have to learn to read at home, while the other kids were having a blast in the kindergarten classroom. Boy, did I learn, and when I finally was ready to attend first grade, I was helping the teacher instruct the other kids in the reading basics. So you can see why picking up copy and just reading it became my specialty.

I started making demo tapes during those years I was in college. Crude as they were, and certainly not good quality, I sent tapes out to production companies, small ad agencies, any place that used voice talent. I found that recording narrations seemed to make the most sense for me. In fact, my early voice-over days were filled with how-to narrations that were usually of a technical nature. I've narrated many training films, ranging from computer technique to decorating tips. I've also done a fair amount of medical narrations.

When I started working at 106.7 Lite-FM (at a tender young age, I might add!), I found that I had instant credibility in the market and was able to interview at talent agencies with ease. But the truth is that I spent many years without an agent and did just fine. I was extremely lucky because by working on the air in New York, I was essentially auditioning every day. After being on the radio at night for a year or two, I received a phone call from a producer at CBS News. She was an avid listener and a radio fan and she wanted to use a woman on a promo for WCBS-TV. I went in and auditioned and wound up doing daily promos at CBS Television for several years. From that job, since producers move around, I also got work at HBO, Cinemax, Lifetime, NBC—well, you get the picture. I started to develop an incredible portfolio of clients from that one gig at CBS, and TV promos became my specialty. The first producer who hired me still remains a close friend. And I am forever indebted to Jana Polsky for taking a chance on me. So during the early days of promos, I was working entirely without an agent, but in time I realized that having a representative would be a good idea. I went with TRH initially, then ICM, and am now with Don Buchwald.

I never really sell myself anymore. I leave that up to the agents, but if I *had* to promote myself, I would use the words *professional, hard worker, good cold reader, warm, approachable, newsy,* and *authoritative.* Working with top producers at the networks was a great deal of fun. But it often ends as quickly as it begins. It was difficult the first time I lost a big account. It just ended because it was time to change voices. It was nothing personal. I lost a great deal of income, but more importantly, I lost the companionship of the little group of talent, producers, and engineers that had been working together. We celebrated birthdays and warm times and we enjoyed ourselves while working those recording sessions. Of course, we were greatly saddened when "that ole gang of mine" broke up. My bank account was greatly saddened, too. But that experience was a vital one for me for I realized that my fate would always be determined by unknown people making decisions in boardrooms at the networks. That didn't sit well with me, and that's when I started thinking about taking control of my own destiny and creating my own projects that I would be responsible for. More on that later.

In addition to promos, I've recorded many different types of things, such as TV and radio commercials, video news releases, movie trailers, game show opens, and even shows in Japan. I narrated a program about Hillary Clinton for NBC, recorded voice-overs for animation, and was delighted to record a speech for Tipper Gore, which she used to study and to deliver according to my inflection and cadence!

Rejection is part of the business and, although it always hurts, by this time it has become par for the course. You just know that it happens and are surprised when it doesn't. Finding work these days is much more difficult than it used to be. I had wall-to-wall recording sessions five to ten years ago, but things have changed drastically. Whether it's the economy, fallout from the strike, 9/11, or just that I have gone through the shelf life of a voice-over artist, the outcome remains the same. I am not as busy as I used to be. But I always say there's a reason for everything. And by not spending my days in a studio, I have the time to pursue other passions and work on controlling my destiny that I spoke about earlier. In the past five years, I've co-written and performed in a play, gotten involved with the food industry, and am in the process of producing a meditation CD. I've hosted and interviewed many superstar artists for the shows. Most recently, along with my production company, Two Sides of a Coin, and business partner, Amy Coleman, I've conceived, hosted, and produced several live events ranging from "The Good News About Cancer" to "One Wicked Night with Stephen Schwartz." Also, I write and deliver speeches to various groups about patient advocacy and cancer awareness, having been touched by the disease. This leads me to host many live events. So, once again, I'm using my voice in a different way.

I can't tell you how many people ask for my help to get into the voice-over industry. I say the same thing to everyone: It's a very tough business, but if it's something you really want to do, you have to work for it. You have to do your homework. You have to spend time and money. And what I discover almost all the time is that the individual never follows through. Having a good voice just is not enough.

I'd love my voice to be remembered as one that provided comfort, humor, and insight to those who heard me on the radio, and for those who heard me on a voice-over as a voice that was striking and stood out. If I were heard on a narration, hopefully my voice would be remembered as one that taught the listener something.

I've had a recurring nightmare that chills me to the bone. In this terrifying dream, I can no longer speak, because my voice is frozen with fear. I know the significance of the dream is the importance of expression. For me, my identity is tied to my voice. But having a voice in a larger sense, having the ability to express and to be heard as an individual, is really the most crucial element of all.

10th SECRET

Be prepared for a very tough and competitive business. You have to do your homework. You have to spend time and money to become successful.

Rodd Houston

Rodd Houston is known for his vocal versatility. He is the voice of the NFL on CBS and ABC College Sports. Continuous clients include BET, Animal Planet, Cinemax, ESPN, Comedy Central, and VH1. He has voiced numerous commercial products, including Western Union, Rolaids, Pontiac, Black & Decker, and Burger King.

BECOMING A RESPECTED VOICE-OVER PROFESSIONAL TOOK A LOT OF practice, patience, and perseverance.

My first demo was created with the help of an early voice-over teacher who offered a demo tape at the end of a series of classes I took with him. My copy came from modified print ads that I chose. It was a way for me to do copy with which I was familiar and comfortable.

My first professional work came as a result of the demo I made. I sent out a slew of copies and got some favorable responses from a couple of agents. They sent me on a few auditions, but after I didn't book anything initially, they seemed to lose interest and I never heard from them again. One stuck with me though, and I booked a radio spot after several more auditions. I freelanced with her for several years and was able to build a decent reel. Then a casting director through whom I'd booked a big TV campaign introduced me to my current agency. I signed at the end of '97 and I've been there since. In my mind they are the best in the business, so I feel fortunate to be there.

My agency situation has been constant for some time now, so selling myself to them really does not apply. As to casting directors, I believe it's important to sell the idea of versatility and creativity in auditions. I think casting directors like to see people who can convey a broad sense of character and energy and emotion. Professional conduct is also very important. I relate to producers a lot, having been a producer of music video for nine years prior to doing voice-overs full time. I know what they deal with in production in terms of putting many elements together at once. I always want to try to make my part of their job as easy as possible, so they have one less thing to worry about.

The most humbling thing for me was probably at the beginning. Once I made my demo and got it out there, I got response from agents pretty quickly. So I think that made me feel it was a little easier than it actually was. In my mind, it was going to be just a short time before I was booking jobs on a regular basis. But it took me nearly nine months of auditions before I got a job—that made me understand just how difficult this line of work can be. I dealt with it by continuing to practice and perfect my skills. I also had support from family (who have always been there) and peers in the business. Sharing common experiences with others who were trying to do what I was has always been therapeutic.

Rejection was never really a big issue for me. While the initial rejection I experienced was frustrating, I tried never to take it personally. A mentor in the business once told me that there are 999 reasons why you may not get a job and none of them have anything to do with whether you're any good or not. You may not be the right type, or the right age, or you may lose out to someone who has an association with a producer who just feels comfortable with that other person. I think that most voice-over people know that they're not going to get every job they go up for, so they keep plugging away in hopes that they just get their share. This is a business where it pays to have a short memory. If you don't get the job, shake it off and move on to the next audition.

Again, it goes back to my original training. What I try to do is create the reality of the copy in my mind and work off of that. If the spot is for a beer and it's set in a bar, I picture the bar setting in my mind and try to bring the sense of that environment to the read. Most spots are a sort of conversation where questions are being answered, so it's my job to answer the questions. If it's say, a new cold medicine, I'll picture someone across from me in the studio and just convey the information to him or her. Voice-over is all about being able to interpret copy and personalize it, and this type of visualization helps me do that.

I've been truly blessed in that I've managed to sidestep many obstacles along the way. I had a regular survival job that gave me lots of flexibility with time, so I could go and audition and take classes. That was important. What was also key for me as an African American male was my agents' belief in my ability to do a broad variety of styles of work.

Some people view voice-over performers in terms of a minority ethnic group's ability to do general market work. On balance, I'd say that it's not an issue that's racially motivated. I think advertisers couldn't care less if you're green with purple polka dots as long as you can deliver their message. But I also think that sometimes minority talent may not get first consideration for general market work because they're thought of in relation to the work they did for their specific ethnic group. It's not a right or wrong issue; it's just a perception. It's the performer's job to overcome that perception and make sure the idea is conveyed that he or she can communicate the message to all kinds of people and not just a particular group. That was an important point when I signed with my agency. I told them I expected to audition for everything, not just stuff for the African American consumer market. They were receptive and put me out there, and it was up to me to prove that I could book general market work.

The majority of my work comes from my agency, but I still have contacts from my days as a producer that sometimes generate work for me. For instance, a lot of the work I do for record companies comes from associations I established and maintained when I worked in that business. It's important to place yourself in environments where there are people who may be able to help you. It's also important to have good people skills and be able to talk to people, because you never know where the next job may come from. I go to conventions, seminars, and social gatherings and meet and talk to people. Some of the relationships I've established in those settings have turned into job opportunities.

Personally, my success has brought me closer to my family. Their support has been unwavering, and I'm eternally grateful for it. It's enhanced the bond between my lady and me. She's helped me get work and she's my biggest cheerleader, and I love her for that. It's forced me to look at my health and made me take better care of myself to ensure that I'm around to do this wonderful job for as long as possible. Spiritually, it's helped to galvanize my faith in a higher power. Not a day goes by that I don't take a moment to thank God for all the blessings I've been given. Not that I didn't do that before my voice-over career, I certainly did. But this is a profession that many would like to have, and very few are able to do it at the level I've been blessed to do it at. So, I see it as a gift from God, and that fact is never lost on me.

Be real with yourself, first of all. If you can't be true to yourself, you'll never be able to be true to those with whom you wish to associate. Second, get some training. Anything that's worth doing is worth doing to the best of your ability, and training and study will help you get there. Third, work at it. Voice-over is a lifestyle for me. It's ingrained into my psyche. If I read the newspaper, in my head the articles sound like documentary copy, and the ads sound like ad copy. That came from working at the craft *all the time*. People think the job is easy because all you do is talk, and that's true to a point, but it's about how you talk that will make the difference between whether you work or not. And, lastly, be strong. You will get rejected, you will be told "no," and you will be disappointed. But if you want it, you must persevere. Even if you combine all these things, there are still no guarantees. But you will improve your chances to succeed.

Success, however, does not come so much in the form of admiring fans. Voice-over is as undetectable as it is pervasive. People hear voice-over artists all the time, throughout each day of their lives, and yet when I tell them I'm a voice-over actor they really don't have any idea of what I do. I have to really explain what it is in detail. When I mention a spot I voiced that they may have seen, they're usually pretty surprised, impressed, and full of curiosity about the business. I'm really flattered by that, and I've gotta admit, it's nice for the ol' ego every now and then.

If truth be told, I would like my voice to reflect suppleness and malleability to the many situations and environments that I impact. I'd like it to be remembered for its chameleon qualities and that my body of work resonates that.

For me my voice is my life. Not having a voice is about as frightening a prospect as I can imagine. The notion brings to mind thoughts of claustrophobia, as though I were stuffed in a box from which there were no escape, as if I were drowning. My entire life, and especially my adult life, has been about communication. I was a communications major in college. I communicate specifically for a living. Not to have the ability to communicate seems almost tantamount to being alive on the outside and dead or dying on the inside. God, how terrifying.

11th SECRET

Attend professional networking events: marketing and entertainment conventions. These are a great source of employment opportunities that can be supercharged by hiring a coach to polish your people skills. You can't have too much charisma.

Bill Ratner

Bill Ratner is one of the most versatile voices in the industry. He has done documentaries for History Channel, A&E, Discovery; dramatic and daytime promos for ABC-TV, NBC's *Behind the Scenes*, Court TV's *Forensic Files*; commercials for Ford Trucks, Anheuser Busch; daily news promos for CBS/NY, ABC/LA, NBC/DC, ABC/Boston, CBS/Chicago; movie campaigns for *Alexander, Star Wars, Supersize Me, Cold Mountain*; and fifty episodes of *GI Joe* as Commander Flint.

IT WAS NEARLY SUPPERTIME ON AN AUTUMN EVENING IN 1952. MY FATHER had just purchased our first television set—a mysterious wooden box fronted by a gray-green glass porthole and golden Bakelite knobs. "See the switch that says ON/OFF?" he said. "Twist it like this, wait a minute, and there you go—television!"

But at five and a half years old, I'd never operated anything electric beyond light switches and sticking a hairpin in an electric socket. I gathered my courage, slowly turned the knob, and waited. Electronic crackling noises issued from the set, and an unearthly white glow appeared on the circular glass. A frenetic mustachioed entertainer shouted at the camera, "Hey, kids! It's Your Big Fat Captain saying, we'll be right back after this," and an unseen voice announced, "The following commercial message will be sixty seconds long." I watched, mesmerized as a 1953 Oldsmobile snaked back and forth across the screen, and I counted the seconds. As the car dissolved into another commercial, I sprinted into our kitchen.

"Mom, I know what a minute is!" She looked puzzled. "The man on TV told me—and he was invisible!"

Thus began my long and circuitous path toward a career in voice-overs, through the advent of Top Forty radio with Elvis, The Everly Brothers, The Platters, and secret nights of listening to Wolfman Jack and the occasional episode of *Fibber McGee's Closet* on my transistor radio.

An uncle, Robert Jellison, played Bobby the Bellboy on the Hollywood episodes of *I Love Lucy* and was a character actor in such radio dramas as *The Shadow*. At the UCLA Film, TV & Radio Archives, a blind archivist named Ron Staley retrieved a twelve-inch transcription of an episode of *Harbor Detective* and informed me, "Your uncle performed the longest death scene in all of serial dramatic radio." He dropped the needle on the disk.

"All right, you rat, I'm gonna drill ya!" Gunshots were followed by the sound of my Uncle Bobby falling to the ground gurgling, growling, and wheezing for nearly a minute before his final rattling breath and the swell of dramatic stringed music.

All of this has honed my ear to the magic and eccentric power of voices. I began acting in the theater in Minneapolis at age twenty-two. It was the nineteen-sixties, and doing commercial work was akin to signing a pact with the devil. I moved to San Francisco in 1973, and while laboring away in a telephone boiler room for Dial-America Marketing, a customer asked me, "Are you on the radio?"

"No," I demurred.

"Well, you should be," he offered curtly.

There are only so many hints a performer will get from the world; cryptic and indirect though they may be, it's important to take them seriously.

So I applied for a phone sales job at K-Kiss 99AM, Pittsburg, California. When the sales manager asked if I was interested, for the first time in my life I felt like I could bargain. "I'll work for you if I can announce and produce the spots I sell," I said. To my amazement he agreed.

California had a prolonged drought that year, and as I dialed away day after day I settled upon a hook: "I'd like to offer you the special drought package of radio spots."

"What are they?" the first customer asked.

I had no idea, but I blurted out, "A professional announcer will read excerpts of John Steinbeck's *Grapes of Wrath* on our station, and your company will sponsor the reading."

After a long doubtful silence he said, "Sure, why not."

I was on my way.

Professionally I was a relative late comer to the voice-over business, not earning any actual cash until the age of twenty-eight, but I worked in high school as an errand boy at advertising agencies, dabbled in amateur radio as a kid, and eventually attended film school—all of which put some spring in my step toward a voice-over career.

I made my first voice-over tape in the closet of my Berkeley, California studio apartment on a cassette tape recorder. I'd telephoned a few ad agencies, most of which were too busy to send a fledgling voice-over kid any copy, but one writer took pity on me and mailed me some Chevrolet copy. The rest I clipped out of the newspaper and an old issue of *People Magazine*. I got three copies of the demo made and took one to the Brebner Agency in San Francisco. They took me on with the proviso that I make another voice-over demo, but by that time I was doing a midday easy-listening radio show on K-Kiss and didn't have time for such frivolity.

I realized voice-over was a specialty I wanted to move into when a salesman at the radio station named Ralph Pizella said, "You know the guy on the Thrifty Drug commercial you just cut fifty-five local tags for? He made nearly three hundred dollars for voicing that spot, and you made your measly hourly staff-announcer rate!" Through Ralph I learned about voice-over workshops, and when I moved to Los Angeles in 1978 I got in touch with Johnny Rabbit (a.k.a. Don DiPietro.) Rabbit had been Dick Clark's number one radio station programmer and a big-time disc jockey. And it seemed that nearly everyone who was anyone in the voice-over world in Los Angeles had dropped by Rabbit's workshop. As avid as a med student working through an internship and residency, I enlisted in nearly every available voice-over workshop in Hollywood.

Just before I'd left the radio station, I'd cut myself a voice-over demo consisting of local beauty parlor spots and promos for the Concord Jazz Festival, and it got me a job doing voice-over bumpers for an ABC-TV special. I said my four lines before the host, Jeff Bridges, and signed the AFTRA paperwork. As I exited, Jeff said, "Nice voice, man," and I thought: *The gods have spoken . . . again.*

Later that week I picked up a copy of *Rolling Stone Magazine*, and there was a pre-air review of the show *Heroes of Rock 'n' Roll*, produced by Andrew Solt and Malcolm Leo. *Rolling Stone* loved it. Suddenly I realized that this was a once-in-a-lifetime promotional opportunity, so I went to World Book & News on Hollywood Boulevard and scooped up advertising and broadcast magazines. *Variety* and *Hollywood Reporter*–the two bibles of Hollywood hype with the most influential show business subscriber base of any magazines in the world–had reasonable display ad rates and ran glitzy four-color ads for films up for Oscar consideration, and cheesy black and white headshots of actors.

I had a friend photograph me lying down on a blank white background in a pair of jeans, boots, and a t-shirt, with my head resting on my hand, and I wrote the copy: "Looks relaxed, doesn't he? Well, when this guy stands up to a microphone he works and works right. Listen for him Friday night on ABC-TV!" I ran a half-page ad in *Commercials Monthly Magazine* and business card-sized ads in *Variety, Hollywood Reporter, Advertising Age,* and *Adweek.*

Instead of scowling, as I'd expected him to do, Johnny Rabbit said, "Hey, man, what a great ad!" I had fought the fear and self-conscious loathing every performer carries within and had done the right thing. As a result, a film producer hired me for a movie voice-over, and two L.A. voice-over agents called. Each began the conversation with, "So who signed you?" I tried not to reveal my true-green naive Midwestern self, made appointments with both, and signed with Don Pitts, head of the voice-over department of Abrams-Rubaloff agency in West Hollywood. Don auditioned me on terrific national voice-over copy virtually every day for two months; I didn't book anything, and he stopped calling me in. I had the voice, but I hadn't developed the chops.

A friend directed me to a new voice-over agent, Dona Davies, of the Buckeye Agency. When I met her, the interview consisted of her talking at me incessantly and my uttering, "Wow," and "Hmmm," and "Gee, that's fascinating." That must have been the right thing to do, because she signed me, and slowly but surely I began to work.

My first contact with my union, AFTRA (American Federation of TV and Radio Artists), was when I attempted to organize a non-union beautiful-music station in Beverly Hills and get union wages and medical benefits. AFTRA was extremely helpful, and the more I've gotten to know union staff, execs, and elected leadership, the more certain I am that without AFTRA and SAG to negotiate our wages and health and pension benefits for us, the ad agencies, film studios, and TV networks would sell us so far up the creek we wouldn't even have anything to paddle. Non-union voice-over gigs may look tempting, but compare non-union money to union scale plus re-use payments plus health and pension benefits, and you'll see a dramatic difference. Also word that you're a non-union performer gets around fast, and you're seen as second-rate.

One bit of wisdom that educated me about the mind of the media executive is a brochure published by Campbell-Mithun Advertising in Minneapolis that I read when I worked there in high school. *How I Got My First Job in Advertising,* a tiny, unimpressive-looking booklet with ten stories by C-M's top executives, recounted their tales of showing up over and over until the resistant employers were worn down and they got their first jobs. But I was now in Hollywood where employers had been besieged by generations of tricky relentless wannabes. Plus I didn't have the stomach to show up in person and be told to move on. So I became a direct mail maven. In the '60s, I had been a student transcendental meditator, so now every package I sent out was hand-addressed and decorated tastefully with an interesting stamp. Before dropping it in the mailbox I held each envelope to my brow, closed my eyes, and blessed it with a gentle command for the recipient to open it and follow its instructions: *Hire me.* Every time I followed my instincts to write and spin a new campaign—from tiny display ads in *Variety* to postcards to carefully designed mass-mailings of voice-over demos—it more than paid for itself. I became a one-man promotional machine—for me.

This instinct has paid off a million-fold. I am an actor but I'm also a small businessman. I employ myself. I also employ agents, and I couldn't have gotten where I am without my terrific agents. But it's taken a few painful lessons to learn to keep my mouth if not exactly shut, at least operating with some discretion. Our business is the classic small town. Agents prefer low-maintenance, loyal clients who don't necessarily seek the agent's approval for every micro-change, but they get nervous when their clients turn out to be more aggressive at marketing than they are.

For many years I saw my agent as a god in the great Hollywood pantheon until I hit a slump and realized that agents will work for you when you're hot, but when the inevitable "not" period occurs, they often stop. And that was the point when I knew that my relationship with my longtime agent was over. The experience was a real comeuppance, and I had to act quickly to shore up my career. That's when you have to realize that your talent doesn't go away and that you're in charge of your own artistic and commercial destiny. I began interviewing agents on both coasts, made the appropriate changes, and ended up in a better position, making more money than before.

I'd watched for many years the deeply emotional reactions that a talent can have when a rupture occurs between them and their agent. Fortunately I was able to separate my relationship with my agent from my relationship with my own talent. I'd been on a winning streak for twenty years, and there was no real reason for it to stop. I remembered my heroes: Orson Welles, Hans Conreid, Michael Rye, Gary Owens, Brad Crandall, Ernie Anderson, Don LaFontaine—magnificently talented performers whose careers had morphed many times over and who appeared to perform their most powerful voice work as they got older. I have always believed that is how my career would go . . . and so it has.

I've never taken rejection as a part of my emotional landscape. Conveniently, I actually forget most of the projects I read for that I don't win. And I know that voice casting is ultimately subjective; they like it when they hear it. You just keep honkin' out the hits until the call comes.

This business is not much more than thirty years old, yet it's changed greatly. Back in the '60s, most of the voice-overs were performed by network staff announcers. But starting in the '70s, when cable TV was born, the TV promotional wars began to heat up, and the first of the TV promo voice-over giants appeared on the broadcast landscape: Ernie Anderson, Danny Dark, Mark Elliott, Gary Owens, Chuck Riley, and Don LaFontaine, who were hired for their unique, powerful, signature voices that were utilized to brand the networks. I and many others learned our craft listening to them, and we rode into the business on their coattails.

Today I make my living voicing TV promos, movie trailers, commercials, documentary narrations, infomercials, and the occasional cartoon and video game. One of the wonderful things about voice-over is the invisibility. I'm not a celebrity, nor will I ever be. And because of the plethora of networks, stations, syndicators, ad agencies, and production houses, most of whom have no idea who I am, I can forever be "discovered," even at age fifty-seven.

Teachers have been a tremendous help to me over the years. I've studied with so many: Daws Butler, Marice Tobias, Natalie Core-O'Hare, Michael Bell, Arlin Miller. It's taken me years to retain what these masters have tried to teach me: Talk to one person, don't fake it, don't read it, just say it, and so forth. I owe so much to Daws' and Marice's deceptively simple techniques of putting slash marks between the words to slow you down, to get you to discern the shape and structure that the copywriter has created.

A well-used voice begins to slowly assimilate itself into the aural landscape of America, so the more you get hired, the more you get hired. "Oh yeah, that voice," they'll say. One's voice creeps into the collective aural consciousness of the culture, an honorable place, an invisible stardom, a membership in the Pantheon of Voices. I'm honored to do this work. It's the collective purring of the American media mind that occasionally performs conscionable, constructive acts of informing, suggesting, and, at base, entertaining.

One of the most satisfying postscripts to my career is that my seventeen-year-old daughter, Arianna, card-carrying member of AFTRA and SAG, and my nine-year-old, Miranda, have both booked voice-over jobs, are more skilled at foreign accents than their old dad, and upon arriving at home after school, greet me with: "Any voice-over copy for me today, Dad?"

To would-be voice-over actors, I say: Treat your craft like a master actor treats his craft, and spend the time. Don't stop studying. Don't stop the learning process—and it *is* a process.

Occasionally I imagine myself without my voice. What would I do? I'd still be a communicator dealing in the medium of words, but I'd type instead of speak, and I'd be damned sure my disability insurance policy had kicked in to pay for my typing paper!

I'd like my epitaph to read: "Bill was a master storyteller. He had the chops of the classic announcer and he could tell a tale."

12th SECRET

News flash! The depth of training required to do voice-over can be mind-boggling. Treat your craft like a master actor treats his craft and build up your discipline.

Sylvia Villagran

Sylvia Villagran is currently the voice on many promos and commercials in both English and Spanish. These include NBC's *Starting Over* and *Soap Talk* on SOAPnet, along with some of the big awards shows, such as the 2002 and 2003 VMA's Latin America on MTV and the 2003 Soap Opera Digest Award.

TO ADMIT THAT I'M A WORKING VOICE-OVER ACTOR IS A TOUGH ONE FOR ME. It's taken years of a combination of hard work, luck, basic psychology, emotional co-dependence, and Ricky Martin's appearance on the Grammys in 1999.

I was born and raised in Pico-Union, a rough, mostly Latino neighborhood in Los Angeles, to parents who emigrated here from Mexico. Because Spanish was all that was spoken in the home, I didn't learn English until I started school. Of course, now I thank my mom and dad, but at the time, I hated being different and always having to work at trying to fit in. It made for a difficult upbringing, because the world was a very different place back then. Speaking Spanish was not a plus, and on many occasions the teachers made it clear to my parents they thought a great disservice was being done to me being raised in a Spanish-only household. My hard-headed, old world Mexican father figured I'd learn English in school, but there would never be another chance to learn to speak, read, and write our native language. He wanted me to be proud of who I was—of my language, and my culture, and my heritage. My mom would say, "Remember you come from Aztec kings." And I would say, "Yeah, whatever." I didn't quite appreciate that ancestral fact or any of the rest of my parents' reasoning until I was much older.

As my father predicted, I became fluent in English, and it eventually became my first language. But my struggle to fit in continued to nip at my heels. When you grow up speaking a different language, it colors your world. How could I describe to my friends how cool it was singing along to my mom's favorite songs of Javier Solis, or making references to my favorite superhero on TV, *El Chapulin Colorado,* or that at the movie theater my family would talk back to the screen? We lived in our own little immigrant world. My family life was experienced in one language, and my school and work life in another. It was the perfect double life, never allowing the two to mix.

Add to that my personality. It was big! I loved talking to people, making new friends, performing, and volunteering wherever I could, but because of my upbringing I always felt slightly excluded, like I didn't belong. So I overcompensated by making people feel comfortable and safe. My co-dependency flourished. In school I struggled and wandered aimlessly, unable to find a creative outlet for my voice, not even understanding what that voice was. Unable to find anything I particularly enjoyed, I dropped out, and went to Oregon to find myself.

I was staying with friends when a couple of us decided it would be fun to take a course at the local community college. What made me pick Video Production at Rogue Community College I'll never know, but that choice altered the course of my life. Halfway through the course there was an announcement that the local radio station was hiring a camera operator for a local cable access TV show. So I asked to volunteer, along with several other people. I like to think that it was because of my big personality that I got the gig, but really I think I was a better bullshitter. I was operating the camera, doing the lighting and sound, and being paid nothing. But, it was fun!

About three months into my multi-tasking, pro-bono work, the station manager approached me about filling in for a disc jockey who was going on vacation. I trained for a month before I was ready to make my live, on-air debut. Let's just say it was a good thing it was the evening shift at a radio station in a town of about fifty thousand, where the demographics were fifty-five to dead. Since the blue-haired crowd was asleep, no one complained at my verbal mutilation of the names of local politicians and the town, and I was hired. I did everything, weekend on-air shifts, sold airtime, production, and the news. I was a one-man band! This time my reward was $4.25 an hour. I was living large!

I bounced around to a couple more stations and landed at a rock station doing weekends. The star of the station was this guy named Bob Jeffreys, who had a voice like Barry White. He could read the phone book, and all would be good with the world. In one of our conversations I learned he'd been very successful in voice-overs in Los Angeles, and I found that it was one of the things I enjoyed doing the most for the station. He was a wealth of information, so I proceeded to pick his brain about voice-overs. I wanted so much to impress him and took whatever direction he gave me. I'd lock myself in the production room and emerge two hours later with what I thought was the perfect sixty-second commercial. Of course, he'd tell me it sucked, but then he'd suggest how to fix it. I learned to take criticism and direction, an important lesson in my future career choice.

I eventually got tired of making eleven thousand dollars a year, so I moved back to L.A. and auditioned at the local Spanish TV station doing the weather. Of course, I knew nothing about the weather, but I knew nothing about video production or radio, so why would a minor detail like meteorology stop me? As luck would have it, they picked me! (Okay, it wasn't that easy. Their first choice wasn't available because her husband wouldn't let her work.) It was her loss and my gain. I was a weathergirl! I was so excited. I was so green. I was so horrible. They fired me after six months, but the exposure quickly landed me a job at a Spanish radio station, where I was in contact with a lot of big celebrities. This time the

Telemundo Network hired me to do entertainment and human interest reporting, writing and producing my own pieces on several of their network shows. Because it was fun and exciting work, I flourished.

I was doing a report about up-and-coming Latinos in the entertainment business, and one of my subjects was an executive at Paramount. After my report aired, he walked my tape over to the executives at *Hard Copy*. I became the first Latina reporter ever hired on that show. There were Diane Dimond, Terry Murphy, Doug Bruckner, and me. We were reporting on hard hitting news stories like JFK Jr.'s new love interest, the O.J. Simpson trial, Burt Reynolds's toupee, and the *Chupacabra* (they left that one to me, since the Chupacabra and I both spoke Spanish). In the early '90s, this show was cutting edge! *Hard Copy* took yellow journalism to a whole new level. To this day, many people attribute to *Hard Copy* the beginning of the end of journalism and the birth of the newsmagazine show. I was there in the middle of the whole thing and I was miserable. I didn't fit in. I hated the work environment, the people, and my job. But it was my big break, right? You couldn't get bigger than this. I'd been a reporter at a Spanish network, and now I'd crossed over before crossing over was in vogue. But it wasn't the kind of work I was proud of, and before I was able to consciously admit that working for *Hard Copy* and all it represented wasn't what I wanted, I became completely unable to function. I didn't realize until years of therapy later that being there, unable to fit in, triggered that white-hot humiliation of my past of not speaking English, of being different, of not getting it. After a year my contract was not renewed.

Thank goodness, I had picked up a lot of extra Spanish voice-over work over the years and was able to land a voice-over agent. Of all the plates that I was spinning, the voice-over plate was what I enjoyed the most. The clients treated me well, the pay was really good, and it was always different. And I could wear whatever I wanted. It was fun for a while, and I was really enjoying myself until I realized I was auditioning only in Spanish. I wanted to audition in English, too, but there was some unspoken rule that the Spanish talent only read in Spanish because my agent wasn't calling me in or sending me out for auditions in the general market, only in Spanish. The first year or so I didn't ask because I was just so thankful to have an agent, but then I started pestering him, and he would always change the subject. Well into the second year I got up the nerve to corner him and ask why he wasn't sending me out on stuff in English. I will never forget what he said, "Sylvia, you just don't have anything special going on with your voice. I can't sell you."

His words ricocheted in my head. So, wait. My voice is good enough for Spanish voice-over work and the many accounts he made his 10 percent off of, but it's not good enough to hang with the white folk? Once again I didn't fit in, and once again I felt the humiliation of the past, of not speaking English, of being different, of not getting it. He represented every small-minded person who had pigeonholed me over the years, but this time, instead of becoming paralyzed, I was pissed. Instead of letting his words squash me and make me settle for a nice Spanish voice-over career, I fired him and signed with an agency that believed I could cross over.

But, alas, the voice-over world didn't seem quite ready to allow me the chance. The minute they heard my Spanish surname, they thought they detected an accent where there was none. Sure she speaks English, but then again, so does Rosie Perez or Maria Conchita Alonso or Charo. How could I possibly speak perfect unaccented Spanish and turn around and do the same in English? I *had* to have an accent. What I did, who I was, did not exist in their world. So I changed my name. Sylvia Villagran became Sylvia Granville! And, ta-da! I was a white girl!

I definitely got more of a response and began booking little by little. But I wasn't happy with my new Anglo identity. I felt like a sell-out. My whole life I worked at integrating, at crossing over. But how do you cross over without selling out? That's the million-dollar question. I felt I had failed miserably. So I changed back to my Latina identity. And then—something life-changing happened.

The Grammys. Ricky Martin. 1999. Suddenly, Latinos were hip, cool, sexy, and, yes—bilingual. It was amazing! I was being called in for virtually everything. It still took some time to establish myself with the casting houses and the clients, but I no longer lost work because of my Latino-ness.

Today I have several accounts in both markets, and I know I'm a successful voice-over actress. But success is something I have a hard time dealing with, and I have yet to make peace with it. No one told me that the fear that it will all be taken away tomorrow and I'll end up selling oranges on the off-ramp of the freeway would still be there. I just drive a nicer car. Back in the day, the fear would've taken over, but now I make it work for me.

Actually, it's that overwhelming fear that keeps me working hard not to have to sell oranges on the off-ramp of the 101, being grateful for every job and every person I meet (even the difficult ones).

I want to be remembered as the voice of the Latino woman. I want to be remembered as the voice that thinks in Spanish, speaks in Spanish, dreams in Spanish, and yet is completely fluent in the English speaking world. I'll make you forget that Spanish is my first language. I want to be remembered as the voice that crossed over, but never sold out.

I can't imagine my life without a voice, without the ability to verbally or coherently communicate. It would be like being a dancer without feet. It would erase my ability to express my life experience, my rage, my happiness, my fear, my culture, and my history to the world. To give voice to this life I've worked so hard to create. What kind of a world would it be without my voice? In my world, it would be a very quiet one.

13th SECRET

Learn to embrace criticism and direction. The client is paying you for your ability to become what the script requires—your capacity to dance in the conversation.

Dave Fennoy

Dave Fennoy is one of the most recognized voice actors in Los Angeles. He has been the spokes-voice for numerous commercial campaigns, including McDonalds, Corona Beer, Toyota, and AT&T, and he has narrated programs for National Geographic and Discovery Channel. He voices promos for ABC, CBS, the WB, FOX, Showtime, Starz, and the Disney Channel, and he is the show announcer for such TV shows as *The Billboard Music Awards*, *Cedric the Entertainer Presents*, and the *NAACP Image Awards*. Every Saturday night he introduces *Showtime* at the Apollo.

ANYONE WHO IS LOOKING TO HAVE A SUCCESSFUL VOICE-OVER CAREER WILL need some combination of talent, desire, confidence, persistence, and a little luck. I came to voice-overs from a successful but increasingly unrewarding radio career as a morning DJ in the San Francisco Bay Area, along with years of training and experience from early childhood through college as an actor. Odd, but it was a DJ acquaintance of mine who introduced me to voice-over.

Like everybody else with a radio and TV, I heard commercials, promos, and cartoons constantly, but I'd never thought about the fact that every time I heard a voice-over, the person whose voice it was got paid. Sometimes you don't see the forest for the trees. Times have changed, and it seems now everybody is aware of and wants to get into voice-over. Even after discovering that voice-overs were a possible and even desired career path, it took me another year and the uncertainty of a radio career to get my butt into gear. But once I got started, I worked hard at getting my foot in the voice-over door. And I did everything wrong.

My first demo tape was bad—about eight minutes of complete retail commercials back to back that I'd voiced for the radio station. They were the typical sales pitch—hurry, buy now, 10 percent, 20 percent, up to 50 percent off—seventy seconds of copy jammed into sixty, with the address, directions, and phone number four times. I'm sure it sounded like one long really bad retail radio commercial break. Its only saving grace was that I did a number of different voices: a Jamaican, an Englishman, a nerdy guy, a big announcer, and a mellow announcer.

Being one of the better-known DJs in town, I expected a call in a day or two. I waited a couple of weeks, and nothing happened, so I made some calls and was told I sounded too much like a DJ and the spots were too "local retail sounding." Back to the station's studio. I had complete confidence that I was great and that with the new tape I'd be signed immediately. I sent the new tape to the same agents and a few broadcast producers. Nothing happened. I again called the agents and broadcast producers, and a producer at San Francisco's Grey Advertising told me to forget it; they already had enough voices in the business.

After a few conversations with agents, broadcast producers, and some working voice-over actors, I recorded a new tape with dummy national commercials, kept the Jamaican spot, and cut it all down to the then acceptable three minutes. That's the tape that got me in the door with Joan Spangler, my first agent and the top voice-over agent in San Francisco at the time. She told me I wasn't ready, to keep practicing, make a new tape, and call her again in six months. Six months later I was back, but with the same tape, and she signed me.

To this day I believe she signed me not because she liked the tape better but because I had the desire, confidence, and persistence to keep coming back. After signing with Joan, I began to audition and booked one of the first commercials I auditioned for. I knew I was on my way. I booked my next job two months later, the next six weeks after that. Thank God I was still on the radio! Since I wasn't booking through my agent, I began to seek work on my own and landed two positions: a staff announcer at TV 20 in San Francisco and one for a company called Megaphone that produced 976 phone entertainment. I was the voice-over of the Lottery Update line, one of the sexy male voice-overs on the fantasy lines for women, and the voice-over of the Michael Jackson and Prince hotlines. Not a lot of money, but I was working. I was also beginning to make friends with others beginning their own voice-over careers—like Joe Paulino and Toby Gleason.

Toby and I lived in the same neighborhood, and we'd often have lunch together and discuss our careers. Suddenly it seemed he was booking every week while I was still booking about once a month. I asked him what his secret was, and he reluctantly told me he'd started taking voice-over classes with Bobby Block from L.A. (She later changed her name to Samantha Paris.) I signed up for her next class and after a few weeks was beginning to book more frequently. The lesson is, whatever it is you want to do, get the proper training. I continued training and took a weekend workshop featuring Leigh Gilbert, an agent from a top Los Angeles voice-over agency. She suggested that if I ever wanted to pursue a voice-over career in L.A., she'd be happy to sign me at Sutton, Barth & Vennari and help me get started.

Six months later I was in L.A. The time between my introduction to voice-over and when I left for L.A. was six years: one year of knowing I wanted to do it but doing nothing about it, another two years of getting a toe in the door, and finally after three years with voice-over as a sideline to radio, an invitation to play in the big leagues in L.A. I'm sure my story is like many others. I have a talent for voice-over, but my success was only realized by the desire to succeed, the confidence to do it, the persistence to hang in there, and the luck to be in the right place at the right time. Luck, however, happens when preparation and opportunity come together.

How you promote yourself depends on where you are in your career. When you are just starting out, and perhaps the first few years, your job is to let the producers know you exist and what your product is. Your product is your read or reads. It helps if you can define for yourself who you are as a voice-over talent. When you know who you are or what your product is, you can let the voice-over hiring community know as well. When I first arrived in L.A., I sent out demo cassettes to a list of commercial, promo, and animation producers. Once I started working, which thankfully was within a month, I sent out postcards every three months or so announcing the various campaigns I had done in the previous two or three months. The idea was to make sure my name got in front of the faces that do the hiring and that they had an idea who the name was that went with commercials they were hearing and seeing.

There comes a point in your career where you're no longer trying to get people to know who you are and hoping to be hired so much as you are reminding them that you are there and available. The assumption is that you've been around long enough that those who do the hiring know who you are. So instead of announcements of what I've done, I now send appreciation gifts as self-promotions. For several years, I've had Dave Fennoy coffee cups manufactured that I send to producers, agents, and casting directors during the holiday season. One year I brewed, bottled, and sent Dave Fennoy Private Reserve African Lager. It was a novelty gift with a humorous label, and the beer was very good. Many who received it were hesitant to drink it because the label was so cool. I still find Dave Fennoy cups and bottles of beer in studios all over L.A., and I've been told that I've been thought of for projects because my name was on a cup or beer bottle. Calendars, pens, hats, t-shirts—I've even seen tiny carpenter's levels with a talent's name on it as in "Can I get a level." They're all good ideas. Hey, advertising works. If anybody should know that, a voice-over guy should. Appreciation promotional gifts are appropriate and a good idea no matter what level you're on.

The Internet and email have expanded the possibilities for self-promotion. I have a website with samples of my work (*www.davefennoy.com*) and a premium page at Voicebank with a link to my website, and I'm in the process of upgrading and expanding my website to make it more personable. One could also develop an email address list of producers and casting agents with the caveat that what you do with it isn't perceived as spam. And you should never forget the old-school self-promotion: business cards, a smile, and a confident "Call me if I can help you out"—never "Please, do you have anything for me?"

In my first year in L.A. I was hired by one of the networks to do voice-over promos for the Muhammad Ali 50th Birthday Celebration, a star-studded gala television special and my first network job. The producer had worked with me on something else and thought I would be perfect. The spots sounded great, and that very evening I heard them on the air. But a few days later I got a call from the producer letting me know that one of the network's suits, after initially liking the spots, decided they should be pulled once he was told that I'm black. Yes, he had to be told. The explanation was that although Muhammad Ali is black, it was a general market sell, and a black voice-over might give white viewers the idea that they weren't supposed to watch. I was livid, but I decided to be the devil's voice-over advocate. "Okay," I said, "so how about letting me do some promos for the black shows you have on?"

"Well," the producer said "even though those shows have black casts, we want to give them a general market sell so a black voice-over won't work."

"Then how about I do some of the general market shows?" I asked.

"Well those are general market shows," he said, "and so we can't use you on those."

"So," I said, "you're telling me that because I'm black I can't work on your network?"

He hadn't really thought about what he was saying. It hit him, and maybe that network's legal department, and for the next several years I was a fixture on that network but never one of the everyday voices. I did promos for the music specials and dramas with racial themes. Whenever a show with a black cast premiered, I did all the promos to introduce it. But once it was in the weekly schedule, one of the white promo voices took over, and, frankly, the practice has remained pretty much the same at all the networks. If you are black, you are marginalized to the ethnic sell, while your white counterparts do the general market and ethnic promos. Of course, there have been exceptions. For many years I was a staff voice-over for the Disney Channel, and there was nothing ethnic about the shows I was promoting. Sadly, I'm sure the people who make these racially tainted choices do not consider themselves racists. I wouldn't be surprised if many—if not most—have black friends, but still they are poisoned by the deep-seated racial stereotypes that infect us all. What do I do? I keep working and auditioning. When a director asks me if I can make it "blacker," I smile and ask "Would you ever ask a white actor to make it whiter?" Sometimes they get it.

No matter who you are and what you do, you're going to experience rejection, perhaps even more so when you're a voice-over actor. Think about it. The advertiser sends a script out to agencies in L.A., New York, maybe Chicago and San Francisco as well. Perhaps two hundred voice-overs read for the same spot, but only one gets the job. It's not personal; it's a numbers game. You've got to be very good and you've got to audition. The more you audition, the more you will book. The more you book, the more you will book.

My process for analyzing copy is constantly evolving, as are the kinds of reads we're hearing. What was great ten years ago doesn't work today. When I began, I used the DJ approach that works great for soulless retail copy, but I've had to learn to listen for the emotion and attitude of the copy, to ask myself questions: Who am I? Who am I talking to? How many? How far away are they? Male? Female? What is the copy really trying to say? Is there a message between the lines? A subtext? What devices is the writer using? These and other questions help me discover the voice-over that can sell a product the real me doesn't use and may not even like. It also helps me to stay real and communicate on a personable level. Voice-over is acting; they just don't see you. After learning to really communicate, you have to learn the techniques for various kind of reads, such as drama promos, comedy promos, trailer reads, or spokesperson reads. But none of them will work if you aren't a real person talking to a real person.

Several years ago I experienced a very emotionally draining divorce. I was in so much pain I was almost numb. Daily, however, I wore a smile and went about my business as usual. Or so I thought. What I noticed over the two years that it took to get through that was that my bookings dropped in half. And within a month of the final divorce, my career turned around. I was in a situation too draining to control, and it had a devastating effect on my earnings for two years. Most of the time, however, we are very much in control of our mental state. I believe you can program yourself for success or failure by what you think. There are metaphysical laws that you cannot avoid. But you've got to be realistic. It usually takes several years to get a voice-over career going. If you arm yourself with the proper training, you'll meet with success.

As a black man in America, the issues of race and its impact are never too far away. The question, "Am I being judged, denied, overlooked, or heard differently because I'm a black man?" is always there. Sometimes the answer to one of those questions is yes and sometimes it's no. Racism is very much like a virus that lurks in all of us. Most of the time it's easy to get along with people no matter the race, and then something happens. The economy goes bad, and suddenly every white man who didn't get the job he wanted lost it to a less qualified somebody else who was hired only to fill some quota. OJ is found not guilty, and the Red Sea parts between black and white America. Generally the racism is less obvious, practiced by people who don't think of themselves as racist. Thankfully, there are exceptions. I am one of them. One of my voice-over heroes, Percy Rodriguez, is another, as is Keith David, who is doing wonderful work for BMW and UPS. And we can't forget the masterful James Earl Jones. But we four are a few exceptions to the rule that usually marginalizes black voice-overs to ethnic products or marketing to an ethnic demographic. White people play black people on *The Simpsons*. None of the networks except UPN have a regular black staff announcer in primetime, and even UPN has now split that work with a white announcer. Lately, it's been mostly white voice-overs doing trailers for predominately black movies. Despite this, I've been successful. Why? Aside from talent, I think it's attitude. I don't show up with a chip on my shoulder. I treat everyone I come into contact with the way I want to be treated. When I'm confronted with racism, I handle the situation calmly and without anger because we are all infected even though most of us don't want to be. And I don't approach auditions thinking I won't get the job because I'm black, or that I will, because I am. If one hundred people audition, and I'm the only black voice-over in the bunch and I don't get the job, maybe the reason they chose somebody else was just because they liked that read better than mine and the other voice-overs of whatever ethnicities. And often, I'm the one who gets the job. Still, I know racism affects my career, but I hear my mother's admonition: "Son, you are going to have to work twice as hard to get half as much as your white counterpart, but don't let that ever be an excuse for failure."

I imagine you could have a successful career without an agent, but I can't imagine wanting to handle all the things my agents and manager have to handle. That said, in the early years of my career in San Francisco, I found at least as much work for myself as my agent did. But I had to seek work in areas where the typical agent wasn't going to look. Because I was a well-known DJ, some work came through clients of various stations who wanted to take advantage of my radio persona. Also, before joining AFTRA and SAG, I sought out non-union jobs and landed several. During that period, I spent a lot of time searching for clients who needed a voice-over and then contacting, offering, and negotiating for my services. The kind of work I wanted to do—national commercials, network promos, cartoons, and narrations—would have been next to impossible to get on my own. The pipeline to great clients runs though great agents. Still, I don't think you ever completely turn everything over to your agents and managers, whether you mean to or not. I meet people all the time who would like me to voice-over a project. But now I have the client contact my agent to negotiate my fee and schedule the session.

Probably the most obvious way being a voice-over artist has impacted my life is in my look. Were I an actor concentrating on being on camera, I probably would not have grown dreadlocks. Were I a businessman, guess I'd have no locks and I'd have to wear a suit. Instead, you'll usually find me wearing jeans and a nice shirt or sweater. Less obvious is how I watch out for my voice. I generally don't shout, as that can cause problems, and I avoid people with colds or flu like they have the plague. One January I got a bit of a sore throat but did a long narration job anyway and ended up voiceless for three weeks. I learned my lesson. Better to lose one or two jobs and get well than to miss many jobs trying to recover.

To be a working voice-over actor today, take a workshop or classes with somebody good. Join or start a voice-over workout group. Meet, read, and critique each other weekly or bi-monthly. Make sure the people you meet with are people whose ears and motives you trust. It's a good idea to include mostly voice-overs that are not your type. Sit down with your agent and compare notes on what kinds of projects you should read for. Maybe your agent thinks you should be reading for one thing, and you're thinking you should be reading for something else all together. Let your agent know what you want to accomplish in the next six months, year, or two years.

Find out what your agent thinks you should do to reach your goals: new demo, classes with a particular teacher, personal hygiene. If you don't feel like your agent is invested in you and your career, get a new agent. Stay in touch with people you've worked for and drop a note or call to say hello. Never ask for work, but let them know you are available if they need you.

What's the most unexpected thing that's come out of being a voice-over artist? All the hot babes that want to get with me because they heard me on TV or radio—*not!* It *is* surprising how many people express a desire to get in the biz "because they do some crazy voice-overs."

I want my voice to be remembered as one that could comfort and excite, a voice you trusted, that was warm and made you feel like you wanted to know the man behind the voice. Imagining my life without a voice is almost inconceivable. So, I'll take care of my voice and hope to be heard for many years to come.

14th SECRET

When analyzing a script, find its point of view by asking yourself questions like, "Who am I? Who am I talking to? Is my audience male or female? Is there a hidden message between the lines?"

Nancy Giles

Nancy Giles's voice-over credits include Office Depot, True Value, Tide, *The New York Times*, Yoplait, Avenue Stores, Lifetime, Food Network, ABC Daytime, *PB&J Otter* (Disney Channel), and *Mighty Bugs 5* (coming soon to Nickelodeon).

I'VE BEEN IN THE ACTING SCENE FOR TWENTY-TWO YEARS AND DOING voice-overs for eighteen of those, but I didn't necessarily go into voice-over as a career. However, voices have always been fascinating for me. In college, I was involved with the Oberlin Radio Workshop, writing and producing radio theatre. Then I ran it for a while. We did mystery theatre and other radio shows.

By 1986, I'd gotten all my union cards and was doing theatre in New York. One show was a satirical musical comedy called *Oh, You Hostage*, where I played a wacky terrorist. Now, mind you, this was back in the '80s when you could get laughs playing a wacky terrorist. A guy approached me after the show, gave me his business card, and asked, "Are you represented by anybody? We'd love to meet with you about voice-overs." I'd auditioned for some radio commercials when I lived in Chicago but hadn't gotten any. So I interviewed with him.

I didn't have a demo tape at the time, but they signed me anyway. I assembled a tape while they were sending me out on auditions, adding commercials as I booked them. So it took a while, but it worked out well. If they hadn't seen me in a show and I'd just sent them a demo, I don't think I would have known what I was doing.

People interested in doing voice-overs might spend hundreds or thousands of dollars on classes to get a really professional sounding demo tape that ends up not sounding anything like them. But I think I grew into the right sound not only by finding out how to do voice-overs, but also by figuring out who I was. The more commercials I booked, the more grounded I got.

But I'm also really lucky. The guy who handed me the card that led to that first interview was from Cunningham, Escott, Slevin & Dipene (CESD). They are my agents to this very day and were the biggest factor in my becoming a working voice talent. CESD is a great team. Their New York voice-over office consists of Sharon Bierut, Anita Reilly, Billy Collura, Donna Mancino, Jenny Lee, Andy Roth, Tom, Rebecca, and Nate. In L.A., my main agents were Paul Dougherty and Kathy Lizzio. And it all starts with the heads of the agency: Ken Slevin and TJ Escott. They are innovative thinkers who aren't afraid to make interesting and offbeat casting suggestions. They are also kind, classy, ethical, and incredibly loyal people who love actors. Their belief in me and willingness to submit me for all kinds of auditions—not just ones calling for black talent—have changed my life, my bank account, and my entire career. And their loyalty when I was living in L.A. and couldn't seem to book much is something I will never forget. More than once the New York office called just to say to hang tough and how much I was missed. I've seen wonderful, successful actors dropped by their agents the minute the money stops coming in.

Voice-over work is a skill, and a lot of people think it's easy by the glamour of hearing the voices in media. But you've got to work at it. There are practical things like having a cell phone, pager, and answering machine that you check regularly, and telling your agency your schedule. Your availability determines your auditions and your work, and this is *key* information so your agents can do the most effective job. Surprisingly, many actors (including myself) tend to be sloppy in this area. If you know you have a doctor's appointment or a theatrical audition, you *must* alert your agents to your schedule! If you are only available for auditions on certain days or plan a vacation that will take you out of town, you *must* alert your agent! A shrink appointment Tuesdays at noon? Alert your agent! Talent agencies have the right to assume their clients are available for work and auditions from nine to six Monday through Friday, unless you tell them otherwise. If you're clear about your availability, you can work together in a smooth, efficient way. If rescheduling is necessary, it makes you and your agency look sloppy and unprofessional.

Then there's how you deal with working in this industry. I have a funny combination of aggressiveness and relaxation not only with the business as a whole and with auditions, but with myself and my attitude. At first it was fascinating to hear other actors talking about their lives and careers in the waiting room, and to eavesdrop about the big ad campaigns and who was at certain auditions and who wasn't. It was also interesting to hear different types of voices on radio and TV spots and to notice who booked the jobs, and what vocal qualities were out there. But too much listening and comparing and competing with other actors can make a person nuts. (It started to make me nuts.) I was juggling way too much information.

As I got older, my perspective changed, thank goodness. I still wanted to get work, but I calmed down and got back to having the fun I had as a college student doing radio theatre. Sometimes I don't sit in the waiting room so I don't have to hear what's going on in the biz. I try to focus on enjoying the audition and will even experiment with my read in different little ways. And I bring along something else to read so I don't get too fixated on the audition or the script. Life is too short to get all wound up about any audition. It just ain't worth it.

I'm still learning to really listen to any direction I'm given, to extract what is helpful and ignore useless information or bad direction. It's important to look like you're listening to direction whether you agree with it or not. Don't get into a big philosophical discussion about don't they understand how hard it is to say those seven lines in under fifteen seconds! No one cares. Just take in the feedback, say thanks, use the best, and throw out the rest.

I try to figure out what works best for me and not worry about what other people might be doing. But then I've been at this for eighteen years and counting, and I have a pretty good feel for scripts and what I want to do. I don't exactly analyze the copy. If there's a storyboard (the cartoon drawings that tell the story of the commercial in a few simple frames), I'll look at that and see where the copy comes in. Then I'll read through the script a few times in my head, and if there are any words I don't know (meaning or pronunciation), I'll mark them so I can ask the casting person. That's about all I do while I'm in the waiting room because I don't know what the casting person is going to tell me about the spot once I walk in to audition. By the way, I personally get annoyed at actors who read their scripts out loud in the waiting room. If you have to read out loud, find a place where twelve other people aren't trying to concentrate.

Once I'm in the audition, the casting person sometimes will have music to go with the copy, or there'll be a video, or information that can throw a completely different light on the script, so I'll try to incorporate that information into my reading.

A year and a half after I signed with CESD in New York, I got a TV series (China Beach) and moved to L.A. Thinking the series was a cool thing and I could capitalize on it, I proudly put a China Beach picture of myself on my demo tape, gave a bunch to my agents, and sent more out on my own. Suddenly it seemed the only auditions I was getting were for Colt 45 Malt Liquor and hair relaxers. Interesting, huh? L.A. was a totally different environment from what I was used to. The town was chock-full of celebrities who were also going for voice-over work! I was out of my element, unhappy, and unsure of myself. I started having vocal problems and had to start speech therapy. And my voice-over career dwindled.

It makes perfect sense to me now, because if you are confused or unhappy you're going to sound like it, right? My L.A. agents were really supportive, but I couldn't seem to book the gigs. I was lucky enough to get more television series work, but then that ended. I was on unemployment and all the while struggling with voice-over work. I stayed in L.A. for almost seven years and then returned to New York. Within days of deciding to return, I started booking voice-overs like crazy. The last two months I lived in L.A. were better work-wise than the previous five years! I think I literally found my voice. I'd grown up a bit and knew more about who I was and where I wanted to be. When I got back to New York, things really took off. When I began network spots for *The New York Times* (I think I was one of the few women and one of the few actors of color that even read for that gig), that exposure generated a lot of work—and not just for Colt 45 and hair relaxers! Maybe it was a reminder that interesting voices, regardless of color, could be used to sell all kinds of products across the board.

During the time I've been doing voice-overs, technology changed the business a lot. My first demo tape was a reel-to-reel, then on cassette, then a CD, and now you can send those MP3 things on your computer. I used to be vigilant about sending out my tapes and carrying them with me, but I don't do that as much since I started getting more work (and since I got older and more tired). Now people can instantly click on my agency's website to hear my voices. You want to continually update your demo with current commercials, but sometimes it's very difficult to get copies of your work. On one campaign, I did dozens of demos and test spots, and I think it was almost two years before what I recorded made it on the air. After many requests, I still never got a copy of all that work. Now I sweetly beg for a copy of the commercial as soon as I'm done, and very often the sound guy will make me a CD while I wait. You really need to tend to career administrative stuff.

I've faced a lot of personal obstacles: self-doubt, fear, racial and gender-based idiocy . . . you name it—I've dealt with it. I keep coming back to two things: that now I'm comfortable in my own skin, and that I have really fantastic agents who've taken chances and pushed the envelope with me. They saw the big picture. They never ghettoized me. And even though white voice-over artists are used for most network commercials, slowly more actors of color with great voices are getting a chance at big national campaigns. And I think the commercials are better and more interesting because of these changes. Don't we live in a multiethnic world? And don't women outnumber men in the population? Why shouldn't advertising reflect this? The door has opened, and I don't think it will ever be as closed as it was, thank God!

There's no longer so much of an assumption that every black person is going to sound like a rap singer either. The racism that's existed in this country has been perpetuated not just by white people in the creative industries, but by black people as well. I've read commercials written by both black and white writers and produced by both black and white agencies that are ignorant and racist, but this is changing. It's not as cut and dried as it used to be.

The gender gap is worse than the racial one, but that's beginning to change, too. These days female voices are doing authoritative spots that were traditionally male voices. The crazy thing is how prejudice could spill over into something like the quality of a voice. And that's one of the things about voice-over that I love so much. You lay your voice down on a tape, and they either dig it or they don't. We women have fewer opportunities than men, but it's slowly improving. But for me, as a black woman, a lot of these opportunities have to do with Cunningham. By thinking outside of the box, they help casting directors try something different. Say the ad agencies think they only want guys, but the agent says here's a girl, give her a listen, and the casting director tries her and she gets the gig, it makes everybody look like an innovator.

Voice-overs can be so much fun with a good script, great people, and respectful producers. On the other hand, they can be a kind of hell when someone wants you to do things over and over again because they know you're paid for. And you can't say anything back. I worked for a hateful woman producer once who'd been rejected by my agency for voice-over work. She was particularly abusive and competitive with the female talent. I was able to get out of that job, and the experience actually inspired some great comedy material, but thanks to her I got a little complex about the way I said the word *premiere*. Then there was this white Southern producer I worked with. I have a low voice, yet he wanted me to pitch it really high and do bizarre chuckles and laughs. He kept reminding me that I was selling to poor people who would be excited at these great prices. Not only were his ideas offensive, the job hurt my throat. A white girl doing commercials at the same time had no bizarre chuckles, no dopey laughs.

My throat's really sensitive, and it's easy to have problems, but I haven't had any now in a long time because I take care of myself. Especially the night before a booking, I don't drink, and I stay away from smoky environments or places where I have to shout to be heard. I also try not to talk a lot on the phone. I take voice lessons when I can with a great coach, Richard Dorr, to help my range, flexibility, and stamina. And if I get hoarse, I'll chew gum or suck on lozenges containing glycerin. (Menthol lozenges dry the throat.) I was never a smoker. It wrecks your throat. And I try to drink a lot of water. Throat Coat tea and Slippery Elm lozenges also have been a lifesaver. Tea in general is great, especially mint teas, green teas, and herbal teas.

I've worked really hard, and if I have a good reputation, I feel like I've earned it. I learn things from every job and I've been blessed to have a lot of jobs to learn from. I love what I do and feel lucky to be paid to do something I love. I like and respect most of the people I've worked with and understand the pressures they work under. I love the craft of putting a voice to words and music and then to a picture. I'm in awe of the sound engineers. It's fantastic to be a part of a thirty-second piece of art. There have been particular on-air campaigns, and some that weren't for air, that I've been as proud of as any of my stage and screen acting work.

Rejection ain't easy, that's for sure. It's just a regular part of our work though and our work-seeking process. And, to some extent, every take you do of a script after that very first one can be seen as a sort of rejection: Why didn't they like the first one? Did I do something wrong? Do I sound bad? Will I be fired? Did I take that direction well enough? This questioning and second-guessing can go on and on. But for me the beauty of doing voice-overs is that you are being evaluated for your voice, and that's it. It's finite. And while one person might not want it, the next might. I've never felt personally rejected when I didn't get a voice-over job, but the times I didn't get an on-camera commercial, a film, or a TV gig I felt untalented, fat, icky, not funny. Those rejections felt much more personal.

For those who want to break into the voice-over industry, I say: Do some research. (Sounds obvious, but many people never take this basic step!) Take a voice-over class, or a radio or TV announcer class, or a class dealing with careers in radio and television. Local colleges or Discovery Centers may offer inexpensive and informative classes and seminars to get you started. Go to a local library or Barnes and Noble where you can sit and read for free. Listen to radio and television commercials and promos, commercials for a particular network or for the network's own shows.

Listen to the cable networks and get an idea of those voices. You'll hear a different kind of voice on, say, MTV or Comedy Central than you would on CBS, for example. Get an idea of what voices are out there.

Listen to your own voice on a tape recorder. This can be very, very scary at first. I'm used to my voice now, but the first time I heard what I sounded like to the outside world I felt ill. You might have certain quirks that you didn't know about. Don't race to a speech pathologist; these very quirks are what makes you "you." Get used to how you sound. Read print ads in magazines; what's printed on the magazine page is sometimes identical to the scripts of the radio or TV commercials. Listen. And listen again to the commercials on TV and radio.

Listen to old radio dramas and dramatic recordings to appreciate classic voices of the past and present. Listen to audio books; get an idea of how to capture a book on tape. Listen to cartoons! Listen to the genius of Mel Blanc, to Bugs and Daffy and Foghorn Leghorn, and to the subtle brilliance of the voices from *The Flintstones*, *Top Cat*, and other great cartoons. There are different skills involved in each and every aspect of the voice-over industry, and by taking the time to do your homework you'll be that much more prepared. Information is power.

The commercial business is agent-driven. They're the ones the reputable casting directors go to for talent. There aren't that many open calls for commercials and not many opportunities to be seen for them without an agent submitting you. So it all starts with connecting with a commercial agency. I've also met people who mailed their demo tapes directly to ad agencies and commercial producers and were able to open doors that way. The bottom line is getting the opportunity to audition and then booking a job. As your voice is heard from the audition on, people will start asking for the girl who does Tide or something. (Full disclosure: I was the voice of Tide for almost three years. Don't mean to brag or anything.) And each individual job you do could lead to other jobs with the same producers, and all your good work can lead to other jobs down the line. I've been fortunate to work for the same ad agencies and producers many times.

I would like my voice to be remembered as a unique voice, a comforting voice, a sexy voice—why not? That would be a gift. But the thought of not being able to express myself is difficult. I actually had an experience like that in 1988. I was in a show, very unhappy with the directors, and felt like

I was being ignored. We were doing eight shows a week when I lost my voice for a week. I had to get cortisone shots and special treatments, write notes, and save whatever throat I had for the performances. It was really humbling. But I still had my mental faculties. I can't comprehend being without them. I already am a writer, and it's been so helpful to do more than one thing: voice-over, writing, comedy . . . There are a lot of ways to make a creative living besides being the star, and doing voice-overs is nothing to complain about.

15th SECRET

Develop your ear for the spoken word by listening to—in fact studying—TV and radio commercials, radio dramas, theatrical recordings, and audio books.

Stephen Newman

Stephen Newman is the promo and show announcer for ABC's *20/20*. His recent freelance spots on behalf of Movado, McDonald's, KABC, History Channel, LaSalle Bank and Zyrtec, join literally hundreds of previous ones, with major accounts for Dupont, DeBeers, American Express, Mitsubishi, Bayer, and Dry Idea.

UNTIL THE CURRENT FASCINATION WITH TV "REALITY," WHICH OF COURSE relies on stylistic artifice all its own (the young damaged voice, up-talk, ultra-cool-hood, and so on), the two main sources for the voice-over talent pool flowed generally from radio or from theater. Of these two, radio is the more obvious; after all, broadcasters live and breathe on-mike, so why wouldn't they excel as voice-overs?

For me though, the path started with plays, wound through film and TV, and ultimately led to commercials and promos. From acting teachers (Gerald Hiken, Paul E. Richards, Ruth Hunt) I learned *presence*; from speech and singing teachers (Duncan Ross, Evelyn Draper, David Craig) technical *expression*; and from commercial teachers (Bob Barron, an ad man, and Dwight Weist, a longtime radio announcer) the particular eccentricities of *selling*.

Having played four or five seasons of repertory theater in California, in 1970 I worked my first production contract, a national tour of *Hamlet* with Dame Judith Anderson in the title role, wherein a savvy, older actor once commented, "Stephen, you should do voice-overs; *that's* where the royalty lives." When the show closed six months later in St. Louis, my wife and I came to New York, and with not much more than a television, a cassette recorder, and a pencil, I did indeed start lifting spots off-air (to get decent copy, or accents, or tonality, or anything else that might catch my fancy), chose three or four favorites, and simply tried to imitate the people who actually did the jobs (they must be doing something right or they wouldn't be working). One of my models, I later learned, was Mason Adams, which in itself suggested I must have *some* taste.

Out of the effort came a modest mockup sample reel. That was in 1971. Clunky though it was, at least with the voice-over equivalent of an 8x10 glossy to hand people at meetings and auditions, I managed to pick up the odd voice-over job over the next five years. As a creature still immersed in theater, I tended to approach ads focused mainly on dramatic effect, with only incidental concern for the product.

Suddenly in 1977, the light came on when I actually deigned to take a class on the subject at the Weist-Barron School. Like most commercial instruction houses around New York, W-B had on-camera and voice-over classes, but since I had been rattling around town with my primitive sample reel, I naturally opted for voice-over. Those two guys, Bob Barron and Dwight Weist, were a gold mine. Barron knew the pragmatics of advertising because of his years with an ad agency (Ogilvy, I think), and Weist, the consummate announcing pro bred in the Golden Age of Radio, was a stunningly effortless technician. The two perspectives radically transformed my whole understanding of the business. Much of their advice was just good, common, systematic sense—do four to five samples, of twenty to thirty seconds duration each (*maximum*), all revealing different sides *of the same person*—but most valued was their total *specificity* in chasing and doing the work. For decades, serious performers have looked down on crass commercialism, but anybody seeing the rather dense little package of tasks required in a twenty-eight second spot could only respect the need for reliable craft.

As for agents, some high-volume performers work without one, but generally those are people active in broader, more dispersed markets. Most people in larger markets—New York, L.A., Chicago, Florida—tend to have someone filter and organize their work schedule. An Old Globe Theater season in San Diego led to my first agent, Maureen Oliver in L.A., but I didn't stay there long enough to give her much chance to represent me. Once in New York, a succession of agents (Bob Waters, Gene Parseghian, and Jeff Hunter) kept me busy in theater; but by the eighties, I found I had shifted more and more to commercials, represented by Wm. Morris for eighteen years, ICM for seven, and just this year, Cunningham, Escott, Slevin & Dipene. Agents open the door; from there, it is up to us to walk through. The time-honored promotional tool is The Free Sample (what used to be a sample reel, and is now a CD or e-file).

In the audition itself, I try to own the copy by *reading* it quietly aloud to myself, *scoring* a few key words and phrases for clarity, and finally seeing what *two or three character approaches* present themselves as triggers for a decent read. As an inveterate pretender, I find hearing myself in somebody else's manner easily sparks me.

Bob King, a very successful commercial player, when he set out to write a book in the '70s about the broad diversity within the voice-over clan (a project he eventually abandoned, when publishers wanted only "dish" on petty politics of the business), came upon a unifying thread among most of these varied performers: *not* glorious voices nor diction nor even humor, but rather a widespread grounding in *music*. Something about meter and melody and phrasing seems to relate to telling a story in 28 (or 3.5 or 8.7) seconds and making it sound spontaneous and incontestable. That affinity for balance, harmony, and a dash of silliness may well offer value beyond employable readings for other satisfactions in life. The broadcast tradition expects consistency and precision within the world of the microphone. The rest of us arty types, who approach work more intuitively, more stylistically, of course strive to develop consciousness of the overall timings required but then aim to forget the constraints. As in acting itself, one knows he's pretending, yet pretends to *be*. For me, the most satisfying experiences have always revolved around that little zone where I hit my marks, but in a care-free way.

Performers who are heard and not seen usually enjoy a refreshing free-dom. Within it, playfulness and spontaneity seem to flourish, frequently turning recording sessions into conventions of otters. This may well account for the regulation parade of jokes and anecdotes heard in most voice-over waiting rooms (quite distinct from the palpable tension that develops in those same rooms, and with many of those same people, when the casting-call shifts to on-camera).

The voice-over business has, over the last five years, widened yet thinned. What used to be concentrated in New York, with 65 percent of the work here and 35 percent in L.A., is now reversed: 65 there and 35 here. The talent pool is broader: In the sixties, most of the work was done by fewer than a hundred people (men mainly); by the time I got here in the seventies, maybe two hundred voices did the bulk of work (including more women and youngsters). Now, thousands participate across the country (regardless of age, gender, or region). Yet even with many more players, per-haps the most unexpected aspect of voice-overs is the fair chance it offers for solvency.

My first ten years in New York were absorbed mainly with acting onstage and in film. The next five years brought commercial voice-overs into the mix, and by the end of the next five years, I had pretty fully transi-tioned to announcing and voice-over work. Now it's voice-overs exclu-sively—makeup and hair is a whole lot easier, and you simply can't beat the rehearsal (not to mention reading, rather than memorizing).

Though resolutely freelance, my most identifiable gig has become ABC's 20/20. Yet over my ten years there, I have promoted various news programs (*Day One*, *Primetime Live*, *This Week*, *World News Tonight*). While I have done animated work and certainly do some zany commercial work, so many others do it better that I am more likely to be tapped for information, nuance, and feeling, rather than characterization. So news appeals.

Also, my wife and I happen to be news junkies who mainline talking heads on all three networks, PBS, and cable, most every evening and all Sunday morning. While the news may get us down, the news business never has. If anything, a news organization's effort at objectivity and com-munication is a kind of reassuring equilibrium. Broadcasters really do *try* to maintain honest-broker status. The beauty in my piece of the process is that with so many other levels scrutinizing copy, all I have to do is render it; no debate about words, just how to keep them alive; like doing Shakespeare without the poetry.

Regarding a worst voice-over experience, I would have to cite my efforts on an extended cassette Audio Tour Guide, motoring around eastern Connecticut. Having developed some reasonably decent chops to render ten to fifty-eight seconds of commercial copy, I didn't bat an eye at tracking ninety minutes. After all, I'm an actor, used to being onstage two or three hours at a time, eight times a week. All too crushingly, I learned the distinction between *ensemble* and *solo*, between sprinting and long-distance running, between polishing and conveying. My diction was the first to go, then clarity, rapidly thickening into mental sludge. Eventually, after several hours of slogging through copy, the producer mercifully offered to complete the session the next day. While I finally limped through (at no charge), extra studio cost still must have accrued. To work at overcoming such deficiency (and I still need to), the best exercise I've found is out-loud reading of whole books (or at the very least, chapters).

The best part of addressing rejection in voice-overs is its nearly total discretion. Fail onstage and the next day a dozen papers delight in describing each miserable detail, and they often reprise the shortfalls in future reviews. Get fired from a show, and taxi drivers can recite the reasons. With voice-overs, we get bumped off a spot, not fired. In our phantom occupation, we swim through the culture, plus or minus, undetected. This parallel universe, while often shaping the perceived world, rarely leaves tracks—an ideal situation for egos attracted to diversion for its own sake.

If the occupation intrigues you, first, *try anything else you can*. Rejection is relentless. As Bob Barron often said, "Those who book one spot for every twenty auditions they go out on are exceptionally successful," which means they get *nineteen* "no's." If you *still* can't help yourself, then *study* the people on the air now (they are what's in demand). Do plays, develop computer skills (perhaps audio editing skills), and teach; work in production (film, news, and casting). In the process, of course, be businesslike and diligent, and above all, remember your own intelligence and good humor.

All through my commercial years, I always felt that the great X factor we performers bring to the marketplace is our sense of play. Even with news, I think that element pertains. If you watch Brokaw or Jennings, even Rather, behind the eyes they each carry that little investment of personal insight (verging on amusement) at all the quirks of the crazy old world. Within the voice of a good announcer, a similar spark glows. The durable voices, those that keep going for decades, carry that vibrancy through even serious subjects.

In an initial meeting, as Ringo Starr so cogently put it, "All you gotta do is act natch'er'lee." Play off whatever the people there are sending. If they're not sending much (as is usually the case), have a couple of small-talk topics (recent shows, shared events, acquaintances, or situations that might be of mutual interest), and, most relevant of course, aspects of the project that prompted the meeting, phone call, or written note in the first place.

Tombstone-wise, I suppose I would hope to have served as a storyteller, a clarifier, an amuser.

Worst case-wise: Deprived of voice, or words, perhaps one still listens to music, takes walks (outdoors, in museums, or in a zoo), goes rowing, or cares for animals. But without *coherence*—who can know? Just cherish each day we have, I guess.

16th SECRET

Within the world of the microphone be cognizant of the importance of meter, melody, and phrasing—balance and harmony—consistency and precision, then aim to forget these restraints.

E. G. Daily

E. G. Daily is known for her voices in many animated series and films, including Babe in *Babe II: Pig in the City*, Buttercup in *Powerpuff Girls*, and Tommy Pickles in the Emmy Award-winning *Rugrats*.

DEVELOPING INTO A WORKING VOICE TALENT CAME TO ME LIKE A GIFT. I'd never taken a class or planned to be a voice actor; it just came. All the years I applied myself to studying acting, and all the years and years I spent singing really came in handy when it came time to tweak my voice in all kinds of fun ways. It was freeing because it had nothing to do with my body. I was the perfect candidate because I knew so much about acting and my own voice and its limits, plus I'm basically pretty uninhibited, so I could go off in crazy ways, sometimes just like a kid.

Getting into voice-over was by a fluke. I played a female wrestler in a musical where I had to be a different age in each round—a baby, a five year old, and on up to an adult. The number one agent for voice-over, who's still my agent now, saw me and thought my kids' voices were really special. And, voila! It's been awesome ever since. And he's still my agent, by the way.

The very first voice-overs I got were jingles—little singing commercials where, for instance, I'd have to sing as the voice of a grape, if you can imagine. I just lucked into a batch of those because I'd done a movie as an on-camera actress, and the music supervisor liked my singing voice, so he kept flying me to San Francisco to do his jingles. The only other thing I got when I first started working with my agent was a radio commercial promoting a singer's album that was a very MTV, hip type of voice. Then came Tommy Pickles in *Rugrats*, and that's when it took off.

Most people start out by getting a good demo tape made, but I hadn't expected to do voice-over and was just trying to supplement my income. I was throwing myself into it and hadn't even thought of making a tape. I just had my agent, and I guess he believed in me enough to push me without a tape. My agent as well as other friends recommended Marc Graue to do my first demo, and he was amazing at directing me and knowing the right copy for my voice. So when I finally got around to making it, we used the jobs I'd been booking as well as some spots Marc had me do. When I wanted to try to do more promo work, I went to Marc and quickly learned there is a whole different rhythm with promos. Once I had that tape, I began doing more promos.

Promoting is in my agent's hands; he sells me, and I like it that way. I just do the voices, keep my demos current, and show up on time to the sessions. What makes my agent so successful, I think, is that he has an amazing professionalism and attitude about the work. Every year he gathers all his clients together and has a meeting basically about good work ethics, like showing up on time. Being available is important as well because sometimes the jobs come suddenly. Jeff Danis has great instincts about voice people and he doesn't just hire names, because when he met me I'd never done it before. I think he just knows what kinds of voices or actors sell.

I came into voice-over basically on my knees because on-camera work was frustrating and so slow I couldn't pay my bills. It messed with my psyche. There were so many obstacles to working, like after an amazing read, you just weren't tall enough or you didn't have the right look. "We loved your work and thought you were brilliant, but you're too short. Or you're too young. Or you're too old. Or your hair's too long. Or too short." In voice-over, you don't have all those hoops to jump through. It's more about your talent, not how you look. Voice-over has never messed with me. It's been my gift from God, flowing and joyful. And, most importantly, it's enabled me to spend lots of time with my kids. I have so many other things to do that I love, like my music and my daughters, that I don't sit around and wait for things to come. I move forward with what's flowing.

I never have any expectations in voice-over, but I have so much from it I just can't be greedy about the few jobs I don't get. I move on and have fun while doing it. I'm happier when I have time for my personal and spiritual life, too. I can afford to make my own music. I can have plenty of time for my friends and family. I feel good about what I do, knowing I'm delivering what people want. Voice-over work gave me back my dignity.

As I said, voice-over came easy to me. I have years and years of being an actress and studying and knowing what I'm doing, so that when voice-over happens, it seems intuitive. I just look at the photo of the character, read the description, and the first voice out of my mouth is usually the right one. If I think too hard about it, it just doesn't work for me. I think that my intuitive grasp of the voice to pick is a huge part of why I book. My agent is 99 percent of where my jobs come from. Once in a while I run into someone who decides to hire me. But my agent is *the man*.

I am so lucky to work on awesome shows such as *Rugrats* and *Powerpuff Girls*. I've been doing Tommy on *Rugrats* for probably sixteen years now. It's been Nickelodeon's top-rated series for years. I understand Tommy and know how to move him into being a bigger kid. Being involved in these shows has really affected my relationship with my kids and the school, and being able to be of service in a way that counts to kids! I'm always doing kids' school stuff. They just use me for whatever I'm good at, like Halloween haunted houses. I've thought about working with the kids more in drama, but I haven't really applied myself to that yet. My kids are six and eight, and they're really proud of me; they brag about me. They're very cute. I love the fun, the social life, the limitless creativity, and the *money* voice-over brings!

I've been doing animation for about seventeen years now, as well as on camera. When I'm doing animation, I just look at the character and get a feel for it. My other voice-over work includes imitations, voice matches, animation, cartoons, and TV and radio commercials, but my specialty is voice matches of people, such as on commercials for movies. There are so many uses for voice-over; people just don't realize them all. There are books on tape, DVDs, voices for Disneyland rides—I've done them all. I'm really interested in the movies where you get to transform yourself. That's pretty much my main thing. You can be anything in animation. You can be an inanimate object.

I also work with Tara Strong and other voice-over talents on the Web through *www.voicestarz.com*, teaching people how to get into animation. Big voice talents in Los Angeles, top agents in the city, casting agents, animated show creators, and other people all offer everything you need to know on a CD ROM. Another good site is Pat Fraley's *www.patfraley.com*. His CD is so fantastic. I highly recommend it, too. Pat Fraley's one of the top guys around. These sites are a great, great way to learn, especially if you don't live in one of the big cities like L.A. or Hollywood or New York.

The key to good voice-overs is not only having a lot of interesting voices, it's also about knowing how to act and being versatile and using your voice to make the character sound very real. Preparation for voice-over includes both training as an actor and training with a good voice-over coach. I've been lucky to work with great coaches like Ginny McSwain and Sue Blue. They also direct and cast shows, and, as a result, I sometimes got bookings directly from them.

If you're a would-be voice-over artist, make sure you know what you're doing. It's not enough to have a good voice; it's not enough to be a good actor. It's the combination. There's a lot of competition, and there is a lot of room, but you have to be really good because there are so many really talented people out there who have incredible skills with their voices. They have the gift of mimicking and using their voices in great variety. Apply yourself to becoming really good at it. Learn to manipulate your voice; learn through classes, study. Study and become a great talent in all the arts as they all affect voice work. The better actor you are, the better you are with your voice—well, it all plays a part.

I'd like my voice to be remembered for characters that feel like home, like Tommy on *Rugrats*, like whole people. I'd like people to remember the freedom I have with my voice and the fun of it. I can't even imagine not having my voice. The voice is so much the place where you hear the soul of a person, how they're doing, if they're well . . . I don't need to see people; sometimes I can really get them just by their voices.

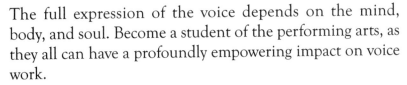

17th SECRET

The full expression of the voice depends on the mind, body, and soul. Become a student of the performing arts, as they all can have a profoundly empowering impact on voice work.

Cedering Fox

Cedering Fox has been featured nationally on ABC, NBC and CBS, as well as on many cable networks, including CNN, on numerous local affiliate stations, on many documentaries, a few movie trailers, and on countless national product advertising campaigns.

SOMEWHERE BETWEEN SEEING ETHEL MERMAN PERFORM ANNIE GET YOUR *Gun* on Broadway and getting Julie Harris to sign my autograph book after her reading of Emily Dickinson's poetry, I was bitten by the acting/directing/producing bug. Between the ages of seven and ten, I enjoyed an early career as New York's most influential backyard theater producer. I employed most of the children who lived on Lakeshore Drive in Massapequa Park. The pay was Kool-Aid and Swedish oatmeal cookies, but no one seemed to mind. A couple of great trees held up curtains, and I performed a rendition of "Edelweiss" that was so somber and basso it still has my parents laughing. By eleven, I was playing Tiger Brown in *Three Penny Opera* at my all girls Performing Arts Camp, the second of many male and old lady roles: *"They'll chop'em to bits because they like their hamburgers raw!"* Junior High Chorus members suffered through my singing tenor with the boys, and my fellow high school thespians waited in excruciating anticipation hoping against all odds that I'd be able to hit the high notes in "You'll Never Walk Alone." Those Gs above middle C were absolutely terrifying!

My voice was always low. The family joke has it that, as a two year old, I would walk into a room and say "hello," and everyone would look around for the person who should embody that sound—say, Marlene Dietrich. They were shocked to find me. My voice was an asset and a liability. I didn't get many ingénue roles, but I was determined to pursue my dreams of Broadway stardom. With an M.F.A. from New York University's Tisch School of the Arts Acting Program, I hit the streets of Manhattan. I landed in a play at famed experimental theatre La Mama, garnering a rave review on the back page of *The New York Times*, but I couldn't live on the $125 dollars a week I was being paid. How do you have an acting career and make a living? I sold subscriptions at the Philharmonic and served cocktails at the New York Hilton until the nine hour shifts nearly killed me. Here I was being *paid* to act, and I couldn't survive on what I was making.

All through my arts training, the message had been loud and clear: *"Don't sell out! Don't prostitute yourself! You are an artist!"* Well, call me whatever, but it was clear I needed to make a buck. I went to visit my mother, and a miracle occurred. She had a party and her neighbor, Eric Weber, who just happened to be the Vice Chairman of Saatchi & Saatchi Advertising, stopped by. "Where did you get that voice?" he asked over the guacamole.

"I was born with it," I replied, shoveling a large scoop of the chunky, green stuff into my mouth.

"You should be doing voice-over," he observed.

"Where do I sign up?" I asked, trying not to drool.

Eric invited me to come to his office to "lay down some copy." I had no idea what that meant, but as long as I didn't have to lay down with him, it sounded fine. Before I went, I ran to meet with voice-over coach Joan Bogden. At my consultation, she said that if she'd had my voice and her experience, she'd be very rich. Joan gave me incredible tips on how to break down a script, analyze copy, and make it my own. More remarkably, she told me to pay her when I made some money.

I headed over to Saatchi & Saatchi, and Eric brought me down to a beautiful studio. I met the engineer who was instructed to pull the voices off some finished spots and replace them with mine. Their casting director told me I was a natural and she gave me the names of four agents to call. Her name opened doors, and within days I was freelancing with all of them. I booked my sixth audition for a national commercial.

Back then the New York voice-over world was a very exclusive one. Because of the timbre of my voice, I was going around with a select group of much older women, many of whom were well known actresses. Auditions were held at the agencies, and we would be directed by the writers and producers of the spots. They got to hear your voice in take one and they got to see how you took direction in take two. Then you could impress them with a brilliant third take inspired by their wonderful direction and your own unique genius! I met people like Paula Prentiss and Bob Balaban and started to feel a part of the community of actors who actually made money.

I made it onto Broadway around this time in a play that shall remain nameless. It wasn't the happy experience I'd always dreamed of so I threw myself into political organizing and the development of new plays as an actress and director. None of these paid anything worth counting, but I didn't care because I was going out on voice-over auditions and, amazingly, earning enough to support myself.

During a trip to check out Los Angeles, one of my AT&T spots came on while I was visiting a friend. His brother-in-law heard it and recommended me to a top agent who offered to sign me. I'm no fool. I packed up and moved west.

The Los Angeles market is very different from New York. All the auditions are done in the agent's office. I was the new kid again, back at the bottom of the totem pole. I got feedback from the booth director, but no producer was there to see how well I took direction or how brilliant I could be. I couldn't book a job. Then someone told me the producers might not even be listening to my auditions because they fast forward to the people they know and skip over the people they don't.

Finally, I was hired to do a promo for ABC *Eyewitness News*. The producer told me I had the perfect promo voice—one with all the authority of a man but the warmth of a woman. I was very excited. Nothing came of it.

After a year, I moved agents to work with Marcia Hurwitz at a boutique agency. I told her what the producer at *Eyewitness News* had said. Before I knew it, I was chosen out of two hundred mostly male submissions to fill in for the staff announcer at local independent station KCOP. After a few weeks of doing community service announcements and movie trailers—"*Arnold Schwarzenegger's got a big gun, and he knows how to use it. Raw Deal. Tonight at 8 on Channel 13!*"—I had a promo reel. Marcia sent it to ABC Network.

I was called in to audition for an *All My Children* promo. I was nervous, which can be disastrous because the voice can't hide fear. Everything you are thinking and feeling is amplified by the microphone. While waiting for the producer to arrive, I warmed up in the green room with yoga warrior positions and deep breathing. By the time I sat in front of the microphone, I was focused. I listened carefully to the spot, dropped my voice into it as best I could, took some direction from the room producer, did it again, they played it back, I asked for another take, and when I left they seemed very happy. Later that evening, I got a call at home from the writer/producer. She loved what I had done with the spots and said that the crew liked me. "You'll be working here a lot."

I became the promo voice for all of ABC's daytime soap opera promos. Then, a producer I'd worked with at KCOP moved to NBC. He called, and I started working there regularly. Somebody from NBC moved to CBS, and I was brought in to voice a few scripts. After four years working steadily at ABC, one of the engineers turned to me after a session and said, "You've just made network history. I've been here a long time, and this is the first time a woman has done everything the men do: promos for a morning talk show, a soap opera, a primetime show, and a late-night-in concert special."

Soon thereafter, I was invited to attend a gathering of announcers during AFTRA's Network Code negotiations. The meeting had been called to protest the proposal put forth by the network negotiators who wanted to roll back the per-spot promo rate to one-fifth of what we were being paid at the time. I walked into a room filled with men and met all of the "Voice of

God" voices that I had grown up with: Ernie Anderson, Don LaFontaine, and Gary Owens from *Laugh In*! I was one of two women in a room of seventy men. I suddenly realized that as a female announcer, what I was doing in promo had significance and meant more than just making cash. More importantly, I learned more about AFTRA, the union that has represented network announcers for many years.

As AFTRA's staff and elected leadership fought for performers' interests, I started to understand why we have unions and just how important they are to performers. I witnessed AFTRA's negotiators stave off a brutal assault on wages from our employers. As our union negotiators contemplated concessions, I spoke up. It turned out that my concerns were those of the minority. Unions represent not only their top earners but the little guys—or, in this case, gals. I was encouraged to let my voice be heard. My union service started at that moment. Since then, I have attended three Network Code negotiations, and I am now serving second terms on AFTRA's national and local boards.

As a young actor, I never thought about the future. I never had to worry about doctors and I certainly never contemplated retirement. But when my daughter was born at Santa Monica Hospital in 1998, AFTRA's and SAG's insurance paid every penny. Needless to say, that changed my perspective as every instinct started screaming, "Save for your daughter's education, her future, and yours; you won't want to be a burden." I encourage performers reading this book to take an active part in our unions. AFTRA and SAG have fought for decades to guarantee decent wages and working conditions, as well as pensions and health benefits. No corporation or independent producer would ever pay an actor proper wages if it wasn't for our unions because the work we do is considered fun and easy. Most of us are willing to act on stage, in film, or in front of a microphone for nothing because it makes us feel good. Those who commit seriously to a career in this industry know the work can be difficult, demanding and dreadfully dull. Performers, like dock workers, are laborers. We deserve to work in a safe environment and to be compensated fairly. As cable television has blossomed, there has been a tremendous rise in the amount of non-union work available to performers. It is difficult to turn down work that pays any kind of money, but think carefully before you take that non-union job. Your employers might buy out your performance today for a fee that seems like a nice chunk of change, but how will you feel when they use that spot or film clip over and over and over and make a lot of money and never share any of it? If they don't pay you on time or don't pay you at all, do you have the money to hire a lawyer and sue them? Our unions handle all sorts of situations like that. They have set the rates in every aspect of performing. Non-union employers know what those rates are and negotiate down. If employers can get talented people to work non-union, what incentive do employers have to pay residuals or health and retirement benefits?

Many years ago I gave up acting and chose to focus on voice-overs because I had a hunch they'd support my labors of love. I have learned to run my career like any small business. I incorporated; I got a great accountant who taught me to be organized about tracking and managing my earnings; I learned the details of the AFTRA and SAG contracts that I work; and I learned to let my agents play good cop/bad cop if producers are taking advantage of my time. My job is to show up on time and to be talented and charming. Sometimes that means making small talk, and sometimes it means just getting the job done.

Advanced technology has brought many changes to the way casting is being done and voice-overs are being delivered. I was a techno-phobe when I put in my home studio six years ago; now I advise the techies. While I love the freedom and don't miss spending all my time on Los Angeles freeways, I worry about the dangers of isolation in this increasingly virtual world. Voice-over work is very intimate. I have flown to meet major clients because it breaks down that virtual wall and contributes to the quality of the work in the long run. If a face-to-face meeting is impossible, I try to bond over the phone. I enjoy being the good news, the one who delivers exactly what they need very quickly. I love the specificity that voice-overs demand and the Zen-like concentration required to be completely present in the moment.

Since 9-11, there has been a reversal of the gains made with regard to the presence of women's voices on the networks. The fact that there are no primetime entertainment shows currently being voiced by women isn't something that people really pay much attention to, but it's my livelihood and I have my daughter to think about. If the "Voice of God" is male in America, then the male voice is the voice of authority. In the United Kingdom, there are more women than men voicing promos. A female producer I worked with from BBC America told me that the airwaves there are dominated by women 55 percent to 45 percent. Interesting. I'd love to see a study on how that affects people subliminally.

All that being said, voice-over has afforded me a fantastic life of self-expression. Whether I am directing, producing, or reading a line of copy, I love my work and the people I work with, including most of those "Voice of God" men whose interests I fight for. Bring your true self into the world by educating your mind and using your voice. This is where your personal power lies. When individuals express themselves articulately, people listen. Tell your stories every day in every way you can because there is nobody like you. Knowing there are stories to be told gets me out of bed in the morning. If I lost my ability to speak, I would find every other way to communicate for I would like to be remembered as a storyteller. I feel especially grateful that this career allows me the time to be a mom and to pursue this dream. I hope that each of you will find your voice and follow your own dream.

18th SECRET

The voice-over game is split between non-union and union work. Take note that most professional voice-over actors are members of the AFTRA and SAG unions. Find out why.

Keith David

Keith David has graced many commercials, including ones for BMW, UPS, and the Navy. He's narrated PBS documentaries for Ken Burns' *Jazz*, Mark Twain, Jack Johnson, and currently for the TV show *City Confidential*. His powerful voice is heard on The Discovery Channel, National Geographic, ESPN, and many more. Keith also is the voice of the animated TV series *Spawn, Gargoyles,* and *Halo2*.

THIS IS MY TWENTY-FIFTH YEAR AS A PROFESSIONAL ACTOR. BACK IN '79 WHEN I signed with Jeff Hunter, my first agent, I told Ted Baxter, who was in charge of the commercial department, that I wanted to do voice-overs. He said, "Well Keith, I don't mind sending you, but it really is the white boys' club." He did send me out, but although I booked three on-camera spots (Chemical Bank and two beer commercials), it took about three years before I booked my first voice-over. It was "Miss Clairol, Ultra-Blonde: If blondes have more fun, what do ultra-blondes have?"

Originally the ad was booked with Adolph Caesar, whom I greatly admired and who was one of the few brothers making some pretty good money doing that stuff, but there weren't a lot of brothers doing it. Now Adolph was in that upper echelon, and we both auditioned, but for some reason he couldn't do it, and since I was second choice, it came back to me. Suddenly I began to be requested for auditions. Then Ann Wright of the Ann Wright Agency asked me to sign. They had a theatrical department, but she did commercials and voice-overs. She was the first one to get excited about me doing voice-overs, so consequently I signed with her. And from then on, I started to have some success in this business. I was with her for quite a few years.

Voice-over was something I always wanted to do because when I was a kid I used to watch *Fractured Fairy Tales* and *Rocky and his Friends* and listen to the voice of Hans Conrad. I loved watching *Mutual of Omaha*, and you had Lorne Greene, John Forsyth, and William Conrad doing all the voice-overs and narration for those animal documentaries, and I wanted to do that. I was interested in nature and the animal kingdom, but I came away having learned something without having to sit through a lecture class. Those voices sparked my imagination and excited me as an actor—it wasn't just your announcer doing sports or some commercial guy giving you information; it was more than that. These guys made you *want* to listen to them.

I didn't have a lot of commercials to my credit, so my agent just gave me some commercial copy to read, and as I began to get work I added them to my reel. The reel ran only about a minute or two with two or three spots, and I just read something as if I had done that commercial. I would practice reading magazine ads and newspaper ads. When I was in school from 1975-79, I studied with Melvin Rose who did a *lot* of commercials. He was the CBS announcer, the voice of Juan Valdez. I heard him every day.

When I graduated from Julliard, we were given a chance to audition for all the top agencies in the League Auditions. All these agents come to see you and then they either ask for you or they don't, and I was kind of surprised because no one asked for me. I was like, "What was *that?*" It was shocking because a couple of guys who I thought weren't the best actors in the world were asked. Finally, at the end of the day, Otis Bigelow asked me if I wanted to come in.

Now from another source I had gotten three other invitations to come and meet agents, but all of them told me they work harder for their signed clients than their freelance clients. When I was in one guy's office, he interrupted our meeting to say, "Wait a minute, one of my clients is in a soap opera." And he turned on the TV right there in our meeting, and we watched a little of this soap. And then a phone call came in, and he answered (in an extremely effeminate voice): "Hi honey, how are you? Everything's just fine. Listen, honey, I haven't got the contracts signed right now, but as soon as they come in I'll send them. Love you, bye (hangs up). Bitch!" And then he says to me, "Don't worry, I don't talk to everybody like that," and I'm thinking, *Uh-huh, I bet you don't.* He was interested in signing me, but after I saw that—well what am I, a damn fool? No, and nor was I desperate so . . . I thanked him very much and went on my way.

And then when Otis Bigelow approached me, he said, "Mr. Williams, I hope you don't mind, but I've submitted you for three auditions." Now my full name is Keith David Williams, but my stage name is Keith David. One audition was for *Coriolanus* for the New York Shakespeare Festival, and another was to be Raul Julia's understudy in *Othello*. The third was *Taliban* in Williamstown. Well, I got two jobs out of the three, so of course I signed with Otis because the other agents were all conversation, and Otis got me auditions when I hadn't even signed with him.

So I've only had two agents my whole career. The first one was Jeff Hunter, and I was with him eleven years; and I've been with Harry Abrams ever since.

Self-promotion has never really worked for me. It's not really what I want to do—*sell* myself. I have something to offer, so I *present* myself. But as much as I have ever wanted any job, I refuse to work out of desperation, so if you like what I have to offer, then we can work together. If you don't, then say that, be honest with me, and I can move on. I don't have a rejection complex. Yes, of course I get disappointed, but I'm not going to get every job I go out for—that's the nature of the beast. I'm not going to be right for every part I go for, but I'm going to bring my best, and if you want to hire someone else then get someone else.

I don't think of it like sports competition because I have what I have, and those other guys have what they have. There are a few of us in terms of type going up for the same parts. But there are different shades of purple.

They can't do what I do, and I can't do what they do. We all have a range, some wider than others. Some people can only do one thing, but some of us, and I hope to count myself among them, can do that and more. I don't like to give myself limitations; I have them and to some degree I know what they are, but I don't think there's anything I can't do.

Sometimes my feelings get hurt, but only if someone is chosen whom I don't respect. You picked him over me? That insults me if I think you've chosen a lesser actor. I wasn't always this objective about it either. That comes with experience. In the early days when I didn't get a job, I had to go on unemployment. I did go back and train as a speech teacher and as a masseur, so I can do all that, and I teach good American speech for the theater, which was my fallback.

Even now, upon occasion, I do a little private tutoring. Once I retired from acting when I had a bad experience in a company and I hated myself because all I was doing was standing in judgment of all these other people, and if I have all that time to be disgruntled about somebody else's performance, well then, what am I doing? I'm not focusing on my stuff. Now, I'm not going to let you make me act badly. I can act badly enough on my own.

One thing about the business never ceases to amaze me. It's that ethnically identifiable cliché thing where when most people hear it they say, "Oh, that's a black man." Now, I *am* a black man. I've had training so I can do different accents or regionalisms, but I've always talked like this, and I won't do those clichés. Very early on, a particular casting director said, "Keith David, he can't sound black." I thought to myself: *This ignorant so-and-so.* I've gone for auditions where the character doesn't even have a name ("Jiveman") and thought, "Okay, I'll do my version of whatever that jive is." Then the comments came: "Well you're sounding a little bit too— can you make it a little bit more locker room, football locker room?"

"Oh, you want me to sound stupid, is that what you want?"

It's highly insulting to think black people only sound one way. Of course some clichés are clichés because some people do express themselves in a similar manner, but media exploits that. You'll find an actor who's willing to do it even if it's not what he or she naturally does. But black people don't really talk like that—nobody really talks like that.

There is a modicum of truth in every cliché, but it's not *the* truth. A lot of times a cliché is portrayed as if it *is* the truth, and that's the problem.

Every region has its rhythm—Boston, Kentucky, and so on—but in my humble opinion, it's just another subtle form of racism that keeps us separate. The funniest thing about that same kind of cliché, as far as white folks are concerned, is that Southern drawl "thang," which is always associated with being a redneck or a dumb hick. Guys like Andy Griffith have made a wonderful career from it, and it's very funny when they do it, but if I use that same thing against whoever is putting it on me, they'll want you to think I'm a stupid country boy. Everyone thinks of the term Uncle Tom as a derogative term. Well, I think Uncle Tom is a national hero. What he did tactically to survive and preserve his family was a huge sacrifice. But the problem is imitators who just copy the form without the content. He had vision, but the imitators don't have a clue.

In an *acting* career—and voice-over is still acting—you still use your body. It's like mask work; you just don't have facial expressions to rely on. You have to focus into your body. As in acting, voice-over work always has a subtext, something else going on under the surface. Of course, you can have some kind of exposition that evokes another color that you wouldn't necessarily have thought of in that context; sometimes it works and sometimes it doesn't, but sometimes you want to make choices that are distinctive and about you. Anyone can imitate anyone else. But make a choice. Dive in, even if you're wrong. And if you *are* wrong, choose something else. It's acting; it's just not on stage or on screen.

In my training I was taught to make choices, and sometimes you have to make them quickly. You don't have time to mull over everything. So you make a choice, and if it doesn't work, the director will say something and you try something else. Now after doing this for long, you find there's an integral tone the material invites that you get better at discovering faster.

You can overthink stuff when you're analyzing scripts and you also can be too expressive, especially when it comes to narration. I learned a lot from Ken Burns. You want to be sort of the voice of God coming in, disseminating the material in an objective fashion that allows you to feel what you feel about it and discover what you think about it. I also think that what good folks do is not completely flat and devoid of any feeling, it's just not imposing life on you. I have some feeling about it, but I don't overemphasize because you can get too musical, give it too much inflection. Suddenly you're not listening to what's being said, you're listening to the way my voice is moving, and that takes away from the writing. Ultimately, "the play is the thing." You have to honor the writer, even when it's commercial copy. These writers have painstakingly chosen these words, and even if it's one minute or thirty seconds, there's a story to be told. You've just got to tell the story without being distracting.

Personal obstacles (self-doubt, fears, attitude, race or gender) will always have an impact and will always be there, but mostly one has to learn to separate personal issues from professional ones. I've only had one major episode in my life where I felt that my life interfered with my work. I was so distracted by my own personal dilemma that it was the hardest work I've ever done. But nobody gives a damn why I didn't have a good day or what happened to me. If you told them, they'd probably care, but you've come to see my work, so I have to honor that. So you get past it. My best performance may be on the saddest, bluest day of my life. Or I may be so full of myself on a great day that my performance is not good because I'm not really focused. I feel good but nobody else does. So I mean life is . . . and work is . . . so you have to do your work. Go back and focus on the work no matter what your distractions are. You'll get through it. It's a great release. Focusing on the work allows you to get out of yourself. It inspires you to get through whatever your distractions may be.

When it comes to finding work, I get by with a little help from friends, agents, and casting agents. In some instances, they just tell me I'm requested. Sometimes your agent introduces you in circumstances you wouldn't normally be in, and you need to be versatile.

At this point in my life there are things that I've done vocally—*Gargoyles, Spawn, Jazz*—and people will come up to me and talk about how much they enjoyed my work. That's quite wonderful because most of the time what I do is visual, so when somebody says something about my voice work, it's like a kiss from God. It also gives me a choice. Sometimes I don't want to act, but I can read books on tape, I can narrate, and that's a wonderful thing. I'm still working, I can still make a living, and it takes the desperation out of the acting business—because the business of show is monstrous, but it's a monster with which we have to deal. It took me a long time because I'm not normally a businessperson, and you can't be stupid about your business. You have to develop a relationship with show business. Everyone wants to have fun, but the work is so overwhelming; you have to take care of your business. SAG/AFTRA—the unions—they watch our backsides. A fool and his money are soon parted.

If you want to break into the voice-over industry, start to listen. Train your ear, because you have to find the voice of the writer, and it's not always like yours. You want flexibility, and the only way I know to get that is to train. You have to go to school, train your voice, train your instrument, read, and listen a lot. Listen to people. As actors, after all, what are we doing? We are reflecting life. Whether in commercials or narration, we're still reflecting life, and everybody else's sense of this is not like yours. Some people are only asked to be themselves. But acting is the art of transformation. I want to discover life and humanity, not always play myself.

I'm sure some critics say I have my own Keith Davidisms but, hey, that's me. Some personalities are quirky; all they can do is quirky. I think I have a wider range than that. I'm often surprised by the amount of recognition my voice gets. Yes, it's like a kiss from God; it's a blessing. When somebody acknowledges my work, it always really humbles me, doesn't embarrass me at all. It's like, "*Really?* Thank you." First of all, they didn't have to say that. And being sensitive to expression, it's awfully nice when somebody says something nice to you.

My voice-over work affects other areas of life in the same way everything I do does. We do the best communication to get the best work out. Communication—the spirit is important.

If I didn't have my *particular* voice, I'd have to make do with whatever I sound like because quintessentially I'm an actor. I'd have to work with whatever instrument God gave me so whatever voice I had I would have to try to maximize that. I don't imagine my life without a voice. It's certainly a key element in my life and career, but every actor can say that, no matter if theirs is a voice you want to hear or don't want to hear, whether distinctive or indistinctive.

I'd like my voice to be remembered as one you'd want to listen to. Like that of Lorne Greene, of Percy Rodriguez, of John Forsyth. Like "When the Saints Come Marching In," I want to be in their number. Ossie Davis, Ruby Dee, Paul Winfield—these are some wonderful people.

19th SECRET

Competition is not the enemy. You have what you have, and other actors have what they have. You may be going up against actors of the same type, but there are different shades of purple.

The 19 Secrets of Voice-Over Success

1st Secret

Vital to your success is how you conduct yourself with your clients. Your personal issues have no place in the studio.

2nd Secret

To gain access to auditions for the top brands, you will need to have a good relationship with an agent. Think of your agent as your business partner and remember, that job isn't easy either.

3rd Secret

Find a mentor who is knowledgeable about the voice-over industry. Trust this person to be an objective observer of the choices you make in pursuit of your career.

4th Secret

It's rare that a beginning voice-over actor can pay the rent by voice-over work alone. Be prepared to support yourself financially while putting in the time to develop your craft.

5th Secret

Don't hold yourself back. Learn to bare your vulnerability and to reach out and risk being great. Think of it as showing up for work at your best.

6th Secret

Rejection? No experienced professional going to *an* audition expects to be chosen for the job. The word *rejection* is replaced by the word *elation* on those *rare* occasions when one wins the audition.

7th Secret

Brace yourself. No matter how physically sick, emotionally upset, or self-doubting you may feel, the thespian credo requires you to turn in a stellar performance when you step in front of the microphone.

8th Secret

An agent is an indispensable collaborator in the creation of your career. However, developing a good personal rapport with producers, writers, and studio engineers with whom you work directly is an effective way of planting seeds for future work.

9th Secret

Don't try to be something you're not, and you may not even know you're trying. The real you is what they want. The trick is to find your authentic voice and own it, be it.

10th Secret

Be prepared for a very tough and competitive business. You have to do your homework. You have to spend time and money to become successful.

11th Secret

Attend professional networking events: marketing and entertainment conventions. These are a great source of employment opportunities that can be supercharged by hiring a coach to polish your people skills. You can't have too much charisma.

12th Secret

News flash! The depth of training required to do voice-over can be mind-boggling. Treat your craft like a master actor treats his craft and build up your discipline.

13th Secret

Learn to embrace criticism and direction. The client is paying you for your ability to become what the script requires—your capacity to dance in the conversation.

14th Secret

When analyzing a script, find its point of view by asking yourself questions like, "Who am I? Who am I talking to? Is my audience male or female? Is there a hidden message between the lines?"

15th Secret

Develop your ear for the spoken word by listening to—in fact studying—TV and radio commercials, radio dramas, theatrical recordings, and audio books.

16th Secret

Within the world of the microphone be cognizant of the importance of meter, melody, and phrasing—balance and harmony—consistency and precision, then aim to forget these restraints.

17th Secret

The full expression of the voice depends on the mind, body, and soul. Become a student of the performing arts, as they all can have a profoundly empowering impact on voice work.

18th Secret

The voice-over game is split between non-union and union work. Take note that most professional voice-over actors are members of the AFTRA and SAG unions. Find out why.

19th Secret

Competition is not the enemy. You have what you have, and other actors have what they have. You may be going up against actors of the same type, but there are different shades of purple.

Afterword by the Alzheimer's Association

George's Family

THE ART WORKS CONTAINED IN THIS SECTION ARE ALL PIECES CREATED BY persons with dementia. Nancy Johnston, Director of Outreach Services of McCormick Home in London, Ontario, Canada, says: "During our work with the clients and families, we are always striving to increase our awareness and insight as to the effects this devastating illness has on a family. Through expressive art techniques, we have learned the joys and the sorrows of our friends. To view other works, please go to *www.alzheimeroutreach.org*."

"We don't have a cure, but we can help."

Letter from the President of the Alzheimer's Association

Flight Path

Ms. Baker's book is among the most unique contributions I have seen to the Alzheimer's Association's mission to cure this disease. As a person whose very livelihood is dependent upon what she can do with words through her voice, Ms. Baker keyed in on her father's loss of this ability as a sufferer of Alzheimer's. This disease is far more complex than just loss of self expression, but for Ms. Baker and the incredible team of experts in her field, it was an opportunity to turn over another stone in bringing attention to finding a cure.

Bravo to these fine actors and performers who have donated their time and talent to the Association. This book has shown me that it is inside of every one of us to use our talents to make a difference.

The Alzheimer's Association is the leading organization in the fight to end Alzheimer's and to support those who care for loved ones with the disease. I applaud the extraordinary effort of Ms. Baker to contribute to it!

Sheldon Goldberg

President and CEO, Alzheimer's Association

"the compassion to care, the leadership to conquer"

Chan Chee 2

What is Alzheimer's Disease?

Imagination

ALZHEIMER'S DISEASE (PRONOUNCED AHLZ-HI-MERZ) IS ONE OF SEVERAL disorders that cause the gradual loss of brain cells. The disease was first described in 1906 by German physician Dr. Alois Alzheimer. Although the disease was once considered rare, research has shown that it is the leading cause of dementia.

Dementia

Dementia is an umbrella term for several symptoms related to a decline in thinking skills. Common symptoms include a gradual loss of memory, problems with reasoning or judgment, disorientation, difficulty in learning, loss of language skills, and decline in the ability to perform routine tasks. People with dementia also experience changes in their personalities and behavioral problems, such as agitation, anxiety, delusions (believing in a reality that does not exist), and hallucinations (seeing things that do not exist).

Disorders that Cause Dementia

Several disorders that are similar to Alzheimer's disease can cause dementia. These include fronto-temporal dementia, dementia with Lewy bodies, Parkinson's disease, Creutzfeldt-Jakob disease, and Huntington's disease. All of these disorders involve disease processes that destroy brain cells. Vascular dementia is a disorder caused by the disruption of blood flow to the brain. This may be the result of a massive stroke or several tiny strokes.

Some treatable conditions—such as depression, drug interactions, and thyroid problems—can cause dementia. If treated early enough, this dementia may be effectively treated and even reversed.

Progression of Alzheimer's Disease

Alzheimer's disease advances at widely different rates. The duration of the illness may often vary from three to twenty years. The areas of the brain that control memory and thinking skills are affected first, but as the disease progresses, cells die in other regions of the brain. Eventually, the person with Alzheimer's will need complete care. If the individual has no other serious illness, the loss of brain function itself will cause death.

Flash Feelings

What's Up with Alzheimer's

Orien Reid
Chair, National Board of Directors

Stephen McConnell, Ph.D.
Interim President and Chief
Executive Officer

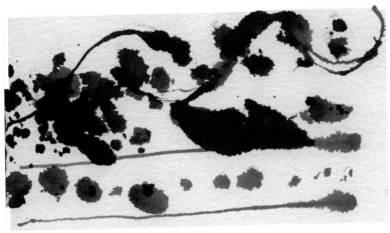

Fishing

WHEN THE TWO OF US BECAME PERSONALLY INVOLVED IN THE ALZHEIMER cause in the late 1980s, Alzheimer's disease had no effective treatments, and diagnosis was an imprecise procedure occurring late in the disease process. Silenced by the mysterious disease, individuals with Alzheimer have relied on family members, friends, and organizations like the Alzheimer's Association to speak for them.

Happily, times have changed, thanks in part to the Association's efforts. We now have well-established guidelines that enable physicians to diagnose the disease much earlier and with better than 90 percent accuracy. Today, there are four FDA-approved Alzheimer drugs (with more in the pipeline) and several non-pharmaceutical treatments available to manage the disease, allowing individuals with Alzheimer's to live more independently for a longer period.

The result of this progress is that more and more individuals with Alzheimer's are speaking on their own behalf. For some time now, the Alzheimer's Association has facilitated testimony by people with Alzheimer's before the U.S. Congress and state legislatures, sponsored educational sessions by affected individuals, and included a section on our website for people with the disease. In fiscal year 2002 we produced a public service announcement featuring a dozen individuals revealing on camera, "I have Alzheimer's." We also developed a new three-year strategic plan that explicitly recognizes the important role people with Alzheimer's play in building public awareness and understanding of the disease.

A new sense of hope in the science of Alzheimer's suggests that this role will continue to expand. Researchers are making major breakthroughs in molecular, genetic, and epidemiological research. More effective treatments and even ways to prevent the disease are now within reach.

There is clearly no shortage of exciting ideas—just a shortage of resources. Although the Alzheimer's Association is the largest private funder of Alzheimer research, we can support only a fraction of the high-quality applications we receive. And even if the Association's advocacy efforts succeed in raising federal funding for Alzheimer research to $1 billion, there are hundreds of worthy studies that still will be left unfunded. The Alzheimer's Association is up to the challenge. We are committed to speaking on behalf of those silenced by the disease, amplifying the voices of those still able and willing to speak on their own behalf, and doing everything in our power to prevent Alzheimer's from afflicting future generations. With your support, we can create a world without Alzheimer's disease.

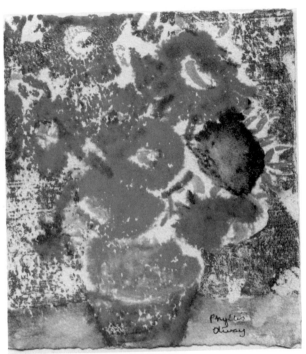

Flower Vase

Contributing to
Alzheimer's Programs

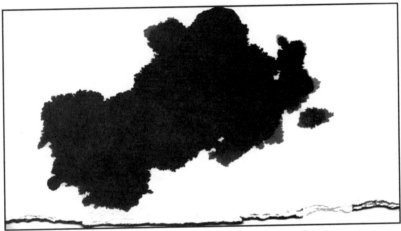

Soul Battle

THERE ARE MORE THAN 80 ALZHEIMER'S CHAPTERS THROUGHOUT AMERICA providing community programs and services. Individuals and companies can contribute to the chapter of their choice by logging on to *www.alz.org/donate*. Your humanity and generosity will make the difference in helping to fund the search for a cure and for the development of more proficient treatments and prevention.

Much Thanks!

–A message from the Author's heart

Information about Entertainment Unions

The Two Unions that Voice-Over Actors Ultimately Join

AFTRA

The American Federation of Television & Radio Artists governs programs that are shot on videotape (not film). These include sitcoms and soap operas, as well as voice-overs for radio and television. Website: *www.aftra.com*

How to Join

Any person who has performed or intends to perform professional work in any one of AFTRA's jurisdictions is eligible for membership. Contact your local office for specific information about AFTRA membership and its benefits.

About Your Dues

New members pay a one-time initiation fee plus dues covering the first dues period. As of November 1, 2003, the initiation fee is $1,300.

Minimum dues for the first dues period (six months) are $60.90. After joining, a member's dues are based on his or her earnings in AFTRA's jurisdiction during the prior year. Dues are billed each May 1st and November 1st but may vary throughout the country. It's important to contact your local office for specific rates.

New York National Office
260 Madison Avenue
New York, New York 10016-2401
Tel: 212-532-0800
Fax: 212-532-2242

Los Angeles National Office
5757 Wilshire Boulevard, 9th Floor
Los Angeles, California 90036-3689
Tel: 323-634-8100
Fax: 323-634-8194

SAG

The Screen Actors Guild is the actors' union that covers performers working for movies, TV shows, and commercials that are shot on film. Website: *www.sag.org*

How Do I Qualify to Join SAG?

A performer becomes eligible for Screen Actors Guild membership under one of the following two conditions: proof of SAG employment or employment under an affiliated performers' union.

PROOF OF EMPLOYMENT

Principal Performer Employment

Performers may join SAG upon proof of employment. Employment must be in a principal or speaking role in a SAG film, videotape, television program, or commercial. Proof of such employment may be in the form of a signed contract, a payroll check or check stub, or a letter from the company (on company letterhead). The document proving employment must provide the following information:

- applicant's name
- applicant's Social Security number
- name of the production or name of the commercial (product name)

- the salary paid (in dollar amount)
- the specific date(s) worked.

Background Performers *

Employment Performers may join SAG upon proof of employment as a SAG-covered background player at full SAG rates and conditions for a *minimum* of three work days subsequent to March 25, 1990. Employment must be by a company signed to a SAG Background Players Agreement, and in a SAG film, videotape, television program, or commercial. Proof of such employment must be in the form of a signed employment voucher (or time card), plus an original payroll check or check stub. Such documents must provide the same information (name, Social Security number, etc.) as listed above.

EMPLOYMENT UNDER AN AFFILIATED PERFORMERS' UNION

Performers may join SAG if the applicant is a paid-up member of an affiliated performers' union (ACTRAQ, AEAS, AFTRA, AGMA or AGVA) for a period of one year and has worked at least once as a principal performer in that union's jurisdiction.

Branches

- LA
- New York
- Miami
- Chicago
- Boston
- Philadelphia
- Washington DC/Baltimore
- Georgia
- Nashville

---

* *Background performers:* SAG is currently revising the entrance requirements for background performers by developing a point system in which union and non-union jobs, along with educational seminars and sanctioned events count toward professional experience.

- Detroit
- Dallas
- Houston
- New Mexico
- Colorado
- Utah
- Arizona
- San Diego
- Nevada
- San Francisco
- Portland
- Seattle / Alaska

National Contact Information

Hollywood

5757 Wilshire Blvd.
Los Angeles, CA 90036-3600
(323) 954-1600 Main Switchboard
1-800-SAG-0767 for SAG Members outside Los Angeles

New York

360 Madison Avenue 12th Floor
New York, New York 10017
(212) 944-1030 Main Switchboard

Voice-Over Glossary

Annc. An abbreviation for *announcer*. Often used by copywriters on voice-over copy.

Audition. A formally arranged session (usually by appointment through an agent) for an actor to display his or her talents when seeking a role in an upcoming production of a play, film, or television project, usually to a casting director, director, or producers.

Avail. A courtesy extended by a performer or agent to a producer indicating availability to work a certain job. Avails have no legal or contractual status.

Balls. A deep and resonant vocal tone.

Beat (applies to reading scripts or copy). Pause.

Bed. The soundtrack that goes under your voice-over. It may be a bed of music or sound effects or a combination of both.

Big. A term used for actors giving too much of a performance in the interpretation of their scene, script, or copy. It refers to expression, voice levels, or body movement.

Billboard. To emphasize or set apart a copy point is to *billboard* it.

Booking. A confirmed session indicating you have a job.

Book Out. A call to all of your agents to let them know you are working, traveling, or are unavailable for auditions or a job.

Boom Mike. A microphone on the end of a pole, held above actors' heads to record dialogue.

Buyout. A one-time payment for shooting and airing a commercial.

Callback. A second audition where an actor is either presented to the producer and director or, in the case of commercials, is filmed on tape again for final consideration.

Cans. Slang term meaning headphones.

Class A Network Spot. Commercial airing at prime time on a major network. Residuals are highest for this type of spot.

Commission. Percentage of income paid by an actor to his or her representative. If it is an agent, the amount cannot be over 10 percent for a union contract; if it is a manager, the percentage is unregulated, but it is traditionally 15 to 20 percent.

Comml. Abbreviation for *commercial.*

Conflicts. Being under contract for two conflicting products. This is prohibited for union commercials. An advertiser would never want one person on the air advertising both the company's product and a competitor's.

Console. The audio board or control panel that allows the engineer to direct the audio signal to the recorders and to combine the various audio components into the final mix.

Control Booth. A glass-enclosed area full of equipment where an engineer and director sit during voice-over, looping, and dubbing sessions.

Copy. A slang term for *dialogue* or *script*.

Copy Points. The items in a script that require particular attention and therefore particular interpretation by the voice actor.

DAT. Digital Audio Tape.

Demo. Short for *demonstration*, a demo can be a sample tape of a talent's voice used to show his or her abilities.

Demo Tape. An audiocassette, audio CD, or DVD recording of an actor's voice demonstrating voice acting abilities.

Dialogue-less Commercials. Used to emphasize a visual image with the spoken words of an announcer as the only recorded sound.

Diaphragm. The lower part of the lungs, filling the abdominal space that supports the voice when actors and singers breathe correctly on stage or in front of a microphone.

Diction. Clear, sharp pronunciation of words, especially of consonants.

Donut. A type of spot that has prerecorded material at the beginning and at the end with a hole in the middle for the voice part. The parts can be reversed as well, with the voice being the donut and the pre-recorded material in the hole.

Dub. An audio or video copy, also called a *dupe* (short for duplicate).

Engineer. Individual who operates studio equipment during a recording.

First Refusal. A request to hold an actor for a given day. It is not binding for either the producer or you. It is more of a sign of interest than an availability request and it is not as good as a booking.

Flap. In animation, movement of the mouth. If the talking stops and the character's mouth keeps moving, an actor will be called in to add either internally, at the beginning, or at the end of the line so that the mouth flaps match the rhythm of the speech.

Hot Mike. A microphone that is turned on.

House CD/Tape. A voice demo tape that includes short samples of all talent represented by a certain agent.

In the Can. When a good take is achieved, it is considered ready for processing or "in the can." It generally means that the director has the take he wants.

J-Card. The artwork on a CD/audio cassette box named for the shape it makes when folded to fit in the box.

Larynx. The human voice box containing the vocal chords.

Laundry List. A long series of copy points in a script. The object for the talent is to read the points with varying emphasis so they don't sound like a list.

Mike. Attaching a wireless transmitter to an actor's body or clothes to record.

Mouth Noise. Also known as *clicks and pops*. A dry mouth produces much more mouth noise than a damp one. Cigarette smoking also contributes to a dry mouth. The less mouth noise you have, the less editing has to be done later.

Must Join. A situation in which an actor has used up the 30-day grace period to join a union and upon hiring for the next job must join that union as mandated by the Taft-Hartley law.

National. A commercial airing everywhere in the United States.

Off-Camera. A part for which you supply your voice to a TV spot or video presentation.

Parent Union. The first professional union you join; subsequent unions are sister unions.

Pay-per-airing. Monies paid to an actor each time a television commercial is shown.

Phone Patch. A session where the talent and the director are in separate locations. The session must be *patched* over telephone lines so everyone can hear everyone else.

Pick-Up. To start reading the script from a place other than the beginning. A pick-up is usually when the top part of the script has been successfully completed and only the end needs to be worked on. Narration scripts are usually done in a series of pick-ups. Pick-up can also be a request to read faster.

Plus Ten. The 10 percent commission negotiated by an agent, specifically referring to the 10 percent added to the base pay negotiated for the actor. (If the job pays only scale, the agent cannot take a percentage unless he has negotiated the contract to be on a plus-ten basis).

Residuals. Also known as royalties, these are additional monies to actors (but not extras) for film, TV, or commercial work airing on local television or international television stations.

Roomtone. The sound a room makes without anyone in it. Every room has a different sound, so recording in the same room is sometimes critical when trying to match voice parts from one session to another.

SAG-eligible. A non-union actor who is eligible to join SAG by being cast in a principal role, being a member of an affiliated union, and having had a principal role under that union's jurisdiction, or performing three days of union extra work. Also known as a *must join.*

SAG-franchised. Status of an agent or agency that has signed papers with SAG and agrees to operate within SAG guidelines.

Scratch Track: A temporary voice recording used as a guide for the voice-over actor to follow. Also used as a guide for editing visuals until the actual voice-over is recorded.

Session Fee. The money you are paid for the initial day's work on a commercial. It is usually a sale amount.

SFX. Abbreviation for sound effects. Sometimes also written as EFX or FX.

Sibilance. A drawn out or excessive S sound during speech. In extreme cases, the S sound is accompanied by a whistle. Sibilance is annoying and a hindrance to some voice actors. S is a popular letter with copywriters and is found in most lines except the last one.

Sign-in Sheet. Exhibit E SAG/AFTRA Audition Report that an actor fills out and initials upon arrival at a casting office.

Signing Out. The act of entering the time you exit an audition on the Exhibit E Sign-in Sheet.

Slate. An audible announcement of the take number recorded ahead of your read. The slate aids the engineer in finding the favorite takes for editing.

Small. A very subtle performance by an actor.

Sister Union. One or more additional unions you join after the first one. The first union you join is your parent union.

Slice-of-Life Commercial. A miniature play that quickly identifies a problem and just as quickly offers a solution.

Spot. A commercial for radio or television.

Storyboard. A frame-by-frame artist's drawing of key scenes with the dialogue printed underneath serving as a rough plan for the way the commercial or film should appear and what camera angles the director should use.

Subtext. The subtleties between the lines of a scene or in a script.

Tag. A short portion of a spot usually placed at the end. A tag may say something such as, "Available at all OfficeMax outlets through Sunday." Tags are often delivered by a voice talent different from those in the main body of the ad.

Talkback. The system that allows people in the control room to talk with the talent in the studio.

Track. One of the several components of special recording tape that contains recorded sounds, which is mixed with the other tracks for a finished recording of the song; the recording of all the instruments or voice of a particular music section; music or voices previously recorded.

Union Scale. Minimum wage scale earned in employment by members of AFTRA, AF of M, SAG, etc.

Usage Fee. The practice of assigning each city in the U.S. points based on population. An actor's residuals on television commercials are calculated based on the accumulation of these points in thirteen-week cycles.

Voice-over. The act of providing one's voice to a media project. Called voice-over because the voice is usually mixed over the top of music and sound effects.

Wet. A voice or sound with reverb added to it.

Wild Line. A single line from the script that is reread several times in succession until the perfect read is achieved. Wild lines are often done in a series. The slate may say something such as, "This is wild line pickup take twelve A, B & C." This means you will read the line three times on this slate without interruption by the director. It is considered *wild* because it is done separately from the entire script. In video or film work, they are lines that occur when the camera is on something other than you. They are wild because it is not necessary for them to be in sync with your mouth.

Wild Spot. A commercial that runs on a non-network station or a spot that runs on a network station but airs between scheduled programming.

Windscreen. A foam cover or fabric guard placed over a microphone to help prevent popped *P's* and other plosive sounds. Sometimes called a *windsock* or *pop filter*.

Contributors

IT SHOULD BE NOTED THAT VIRTUALLY ALL OF THE INTERVIEWEES, WRITERS, and editors of *Secrets of Voice-Over Success* are freely and lovingly contributing their time and words, with no consideration whatsoever to monetary gain, in the interest of benefiting the fight against Alzheimer's disease. The stories, biographical information, and photographic likenesses of the participants are also freely given without consideration to any monetary compensation whatsoever.

Credits
Author: Joan Baker
Publisher: Sentient Publications
Editor: Linda Nathan
Co-editor/co-writer: Rudy Gaskins
Historical Research/co-writer: J. David Goldin
Donation of Alzheimer Art Pieces: Nancy Johnston

List of Contributors
Joan Baker, commercial talent agency: Innovative Artists
David Hyde Pierce, commercial talent agency: Vox

Robyn Stecher, Executive VP commercial dept: Don Buchwald and
Associates

Stephen Newman, commercial talent agency: Cunningham, Escott, Slevin
& Dipene

Dave Fennoy, commercial talent agency: Cunningham, Escott, Slevin &
Dipene; Atlas Talent (E. Coast)

Don LaFontaine, commercial talent agency: Tisherman Agency

Fred Collins, commercial talent agency: Access Talent

Steve Zirnkilton, commercial talent agency: Atlas Talent

Joe Cipriano, commercial talent agency: Sutton, Barth & Vennari; Atlas
talent (E. Coast)

George DelHoyo, commercial talent agency: Tisherman Agency

Les Marshak, commercial talent agency: Don Buchwald and Associates

Sylvia Villagran, commercial talent agency: Sutton, Barth & Vennari

Cedering Fox, commercial talent agency: Sutton, Barth & Vennari; Atlas
talent (E. Coast)

E. G. Daly, commercial talent agency: International Creative Management

Keith David, commercial talent agency: Innovative Artists

Nancy Giles, commercial talent agency: Cunningham, Escott, Slevin &
Dipene

Hattie Winston, commercial talent agency: Innovative Artists

Valerie Smaldone, commercial talent agency: Don Buchwald and
Associates

Janice Pendarvis, commercial talent agency: Cunningham, Escott, Slevin &
Dipene

Rodd Houston, commercial talent agency: Paradigm

Bill Ratner, commercial talent agency: Cunningham, Escott, Slevin &
Dipene; Atlas talent (E. Coast)

Ah, That's All Folks!

About the Author

JOAN IS WIDELY KNOWN AND VERY HIGHLY REGARDED THROUGHOUT THE voice-over industry and she enjoys performing in front of the camera as well. She is an Oobr award-winning stage actress with numerous film, television, and on-camera commercials to her credit. Joan is also a much sought after voice-over coach. She is signed exclusively with Innovative Artists in New York City.

Joan's professional voice-over credits include the Muhammad Ali Center 2004 Olympic TV Campaign; narrating a documentary about the founding of the William Jefferson Clinton Library, now a part of the library's permanent display; voicing the role of Kathy Brown in a special NBC presentation, The 50th Anniversary of Brown VS Board of Education; and being tapped for a marketing campaign promoting the ABC Super Sign in Times Square. Other clients include: King World, ESPN, MSNBC, ABC NEWS, WABC, BLOOMBERG TV and radio, SHOWTIME, HBO, NICKELODEON, MTV, NBA Entertainment, COURT TV, Fox 5, Imus in the Morning, American Red Cross, Olay, Lens Express, Sony Music, JP Morgan Chase, Road Runner, American Express, Costco, and others.

Joan has lent her voice as the live show announcer for the Vision Awards at the Beverly Hilton, NAMIC conferences, the Annual Matrix

Awards for Women in Cable at New York's Waldorf Astoria, and for the last seven years to the television industry's annual PROMAX/ BDA conference. She has been featured in *Interview Magazine*, *Adweek*, *Backstage*, *Media Week*, *Cable World*, *Jet*, and *Post Magazine*. She's also been on television's *Weekend Vibe* and *SHOWBIZ Today* on CNN.

In addition to performing voice-over, Joan has taught speech and voice-over technique for more than ten years at The Actors Institute (NYC), Acting Management (NYC), The Professional Performing Arts School (NYC), and Western Kentucky University (KY). A much in-demand educator, she is responsible for training a respectable number of new voice talents entering the voice-over field each year and provides private voice coaching for corporate executives and other non-entertainment professionals seeking to enhance their public speaking skills for stage and on camera. Among her list of clients are Johnnie Cochran and *Court TV*'s Nancy Grace.

Joan is now a partner for Manhattan-based advertising firm Push Creative, a company she co-founded in January 2000 with her husband. Having always been a sort of hired-gun entrepreneur, Joan is right at home juggling her performance career while taking on the new challenges of running a company. And her contributions have not gone unnoticed; in 2003 she won three PROMAX/BDA awards for two TV campaigns she co-produced for SPIKE TV. In 2004 she won a Gold Promax/BDA award and two Excellence in Multi-Cultural Marketing awards for a series of spots she co-produced for Black History Month.

SENTIENT PUBLICATIONS, LLC publishes books on cultural creativity, experimental education, transformative spirituality, holistic health, new science, ecology, and other topics, approached from an integral viewpoint. Our authors are intensely interested in exploring the nature of life from fresh perspectives, addressing life's great questions, and fostering the full expression of the human potential. Sentient Publications' books arise from the spirit of inquiry and the richness of the inherent dialogue between writer and reader.

We are very interested in hearing from our readers. To direct suggestions or comments to us, or to be added to our mailing list, please contact:

SENTIENT PUBLICATIONS, LLC
1113 Spruce Street
Boulder, CO 80302
303-443-2188
contact@sentientpublications.com
www.sentientpublications.com